The Case for Character Education

The Role of the School in Teaching Values and Virtue

B. David Brooks, Ph.D.
& Frank G. Goble

Published by
Studio 4 Productions

The Case for Character Education
The Role of the School in Teaching Values and Virtue

Copyright © 1997 by Studio 4 Productions

Published by Studio 4 Productions
Post Office Box 280400
Northridge, CA 91328-0400

Library of Congress Catalog Card Number: 95-071127
ISBN: 1-882349-01-6   (Softcover)
       1-882349-02-4   (Hardcover)

First Printing 1997

Dedication

To Rosemarie, my wife, whose support has allowed me to take the path that has lead to this book.

B. David Brooks

Children cannot heed a message they have not heard.

George Nicholaw
KNX Radio
Los Angeles, California

Table of Contents

Foreword

In 1835 Alexis de Tocqueville wrote, "America is great because she is good, but if America ever ceases to be good America will cease to be great."

Today in America we have far too many twelve-year-olds pushing drugs, fourteen-year-olds having babies, sixteen-year-olds killing each other, and kids of all ages admitting to lying, cheating and stealing in epidemic numbers. We have crime and violence everywhere, and unethical behavior in business, the professions and in government. In other words, we have a crisis of character all across America that is threatening to destroy the goodness which, as de Tocqueville put it, is the very foundation of our greatness. That is the bad news; the good news is that we know what to do about it. And that is getting back to the core values of our American heritage in our homes, schools, businesses, government and indeed in each of our daily lives. But it is the schools which have the greatest potential for overcoming our crisis of character.

When our nation was founded, Harvard, Yale and Princeton were already in existence as theological seminaries whose primary mission was teaching the values of our Judeo-Christian faith. And from kindergarten through college, character education was considered just as important if not more important than intellectual knowledge. For reasons covered in this excellent book, formal character education during the twentieth century was largely removed from the public schools. And although we can't teach religion in the public schools anymore, we *can* teach the universal values common to all of the world's great religions. With that conviction many communities across the nation have recently implemented character education in their schools. When properly implemented, it has produced dramatic results. Drug problems have decreased, teen pregnancies have dropped significantly, absenteeism has gone down, discipline has improved and more importantly, all this has been accomplished while academic performance has gone *up*. That's because when you teach kids to really care about others, they feel better about themselves and they work harder. The teachers are happier, the students are happier, the parents are happier and the community is happier. Everybody wins. There is no question that character education should be an integral part of the entire formal education system from kindergarten through the university level.

Character without knowledge is weak and feeble, but knowledge without character is dangerous and a potential menace to society. America will never return to the goodness to which de Tocqueville referred if we are satisfied with graduating young people from our schools who are brilliant but dishonest, who have great intellectual knowledge but don't care about others, or who are great thinkers but are irresponsible.

Character education will bring America back to the goodness and greatness of which de Tocqueville wrote only if we teach our young to do what is right, to tell the truth, to serve their neighbor, to work hard and learn as much as they can, when hardship comes to have courage, when they fail to try again, and never, *ever* give up. That is character education and this book by Brooks and Goble makes a powerful case in depth for its implementation across America.

Sanford N. McDonnell
Retired CEO of McDonnell Douglas Corporation
Chairman of the Board of the Character Education Partnership

Preface

When, in 1983, the first edition of this book was published, juvenile crime rates were soaring, teen pregnancy had reached an all time high, youth gangs were increasing and pupil test scores were decreasing. Sadly, when these problems were brought to the educational table, the general response was one of denial or acquiescence. "It is not our problem," or "It's so bad. What can we do?" was the refrain from school boards and educators across the nation.

While it is obvious that no one segment of society should shoulder responsibility for the problem, it was apparent that finger pointing was the norm. The schools would decry the fact that families were not doing their job. On the other hand, families would blame the schools. Law enforcement, schools and parents seemed to be at odds with each other, thus exacerbating the problem.

Unfortunately, these negative societal conditions, for the most part, continue today. However, there has been a significant shift in the national discussion of solutions to these problems. Less frequently are parents, educators and community organizations blaming each other. There appears to be an emerging awareness that resolving this increase in crime and the decrease in civility will take a united effort on the part of entire communities.

As this more enlightened thinking emerges, there is an awareness that a major part of the problem has been the decline of the teaching of civility and character in our homes and schools. This decline, coupled with 30 plus years of value free education, has taken its toll. Fortunately, the current trend is to find a way to reverse this course and end this decline. The awareness that families and schools must return to the systematic, deliberate teaching of core values has enjoyed a startling increase since 1990. It may well be that the 90s will be remembered as the decade when the teaching of civility was restored to homes and schools.

In spite of this favorable trend, some still ask, why the schools? Isn't the teaching of character or values the responsibility of parents? The simple fact is that such teaching is **everyone's** responsibility. It does, indeed, take an entire village to raise a child. There can be no doubt that the school is a significant influence within the village.

Why the schools? Because the schools are the common denominators in society. Not all children come from poor homes or rich homes. Not all children come from good homes or dysfunctional homes. There are few commonalties among our youth. One thing they all have in common, however, is that they all attend school. Therefore, our schools have the responsibility and the opportunity to instill core values and character in the children who cross their thresholds. Educators must remember that schools have two primary and equal responsibilities. One is to teach children to be **smart** and the other is to teach them to be **good**. I would submit that teaching them to be good, the First R - Responsibility, will make teaching them to be smart much easier.

We must appreciate the power and the influence of the classroom teacher. As we view our world today, a world of TV, music, the Internet, violence and all the other distractions faced by our youth, we need to find a standard, a stable influence or a common civil thread. The classroom teacher and the school are the thread of civility, caring and stability.

As we enter the last half of this decade, our thinking must shift from a focus on problems and move toward an emphasis on solutions and prevention. We can no longer dwell on what is wrong. Nor can we continue to wait for the emergence of the symptom; crime, gangs, teen pregnancy and low achievement, before we take action.

As educators and citizens, our emphasis must shift toward solutions to the fundamental cause for these symptoms. The lack of personal responsibility, citizenship, honesty, respect, civility and other core character traits are at the heart of our social problems. If we fail to instill these character traits in our children, then the next generation will be lost. And if they are lost, so shall their children be lost.

The intention of this book is twofold. First, it is intended to explain what character education is and is not. Second, we want to present some examples of what and how character education works in schools.

In the preface to the first edition of this book, Frank Goble concluded by saying, "In recent years, I have been privileged to know and work with many scholars and educators. This experience has led me to two important conclusions: education is one of the most important tasks that society performs; education is one of the most difficult tasks that society performs."

To these conclusions I must add that education works, character can be taught and learned, and teachers are our greatest hope of instilling good character in this and the next generation.

B. David Brooks, Ph.D.

KIDS, CRIME, AND CHARACTER

Moral education is not a new idea. It is, in fact, as old as education itself. Down through history, in countries all over the world, education has had two great goals: to help young people become smart and to help them become good.

Thomas Lickona

What's wrong with kids today? They just don't seem to know the difference between right and wrong.

This question, so often repeated in school discipline conferences, juvenile court hearings, police stations, and general conversations, came graphically to mind when the nation's newspapers recently reported that a 4th grade student brought a gun to school and shot himself rather than face discipline for using profane language. No longer is violent crime confined to urban inner cities. In fact, the use of violence to solve problems has permeated society as a whole during the first half of the 90s. Worse yet, while crime has increased, the age at which children are committing crime has decreased. Children are killing children. In February 1996, in a rural Washington State town, a middle school student walked into a classroom and shot and killed his teacher and two fellow students.

Are occurrences of youth crime and violence just isolated incidents that can be put aside as just that—onetime occurrences that do not reflect a broader, more widespread social problem? Or are these examples manifestations of a gradual deterioration of our society—symptoms of a society headed for suicide? Do the children of the 90s *know* the difference between right and wrong?

As early as 1980 alarms were sounded. At that time, an article in *U.S. News and World Report* said that the new generation of American teenagers was "...deeply troubled, unable to cope with the pressures of growing up in what they perceive as a world that is hostile or indifferent to them."[1]

One sociologist, according to this report, estimated that one third of the nation's twenty-seven million teenagers "seem unable to roll with life's punches and grow up lacking the internal controls needed to stay on course." The problem is not restricted to inner-city youths; it also affects middle-class children reared with every material advantage.

"While there is much public concern with educational matters such as pupil reading scores," states Professor James S. Coleman, "the fact is that the available data disclosed that youth character disorders—as measured by matters such as increased suicide, homicide, and drug use among youth of all races and classes—has become a more profound problem than the decline in formal learning."[2]

Some people are not concerned about the statistics. Young people, they say, have always rebelled against authority. After all, Socrates complained about young people some four hundred years before Christ.

"Our youth," said Socrates, "now love luxury, they have bad manners, contempt for authority, show disrespect for their elders, and love to chatter in place of exercise. They no longer rise when others enter the room. They contradict their parents, they chatter before company, they gobble their food, and terrorize their teachers."[3]

As one might expect, many people who read that comment dismiss it because they believe it to be unrelated to the problems our society faces today. What they are forgetting is that the youth problems that concerned Socrates eventually were reflected in adult decadence. Finally, this culminated in the decline and fall of the Greek empire.

The fact is, crime and other costly forms of irresponsible behavior are increasing with alarming rapidity and have permeated all aspects of our daily life and social fabric. Our society is staggering under the burden of violence, vandalism, street crime, street gangs, truancy, teenage pregnancy, business fraud, political corruption, deterioration of family life, lack of respect for others, and lack of a work ethic.

Several surveys of university students taken over the past thirty years have shown that youthful attitudes have veered sharply toward self and away from cooperation with and concern for society.

WHAT IS WRONG WITH KIDS TODAY?

Obviously, something needs to be done about lawless behavior, but what? One of the first steps toward solving any problem is a correct diagnosis of the problem. History provides many examples that illustrate this point.

For instance, in 1854 there was a terrible outbreak of cholera in London. More than five hundred people died within a few weeks. City officials, doctors, and residents tried everything they could think of to stop the epidemic but it continued unabated because they did not know the cause.

John Snow, a local physician who had been studying cholera for years, was convinced that the disease was caused by impure drinking water. He systematically interviewed surviving friends and relatives of victims of the epidemic and found that all the victims had used water from the Broad Street well. Dr. Snow used his research to persuade the guardians of St. James Parish to remove the handle from the Broad Street pump, and the cholera epidemic began to subside.

Crime may be more complex than cholera, but the principle involved is the same: to control crime, we must discover its cause.

The 90s answer to rising crime is that political leaders from both parties now seem to be convinced that the solution for crime and violence is more police, more jails, and longer jail sentences. The first dollars from the 1994 national crime bill went to putting more police on the street. While this action may control some crime, it will have little effect on youngsters learning the ways of a criminal life. Instead, it implies that insufficient enforcement of law is the cause of crime.

This is a relatively new point of view for many. Until very recently, the "expert" advice of most behavioral scientists—criminologists, sociologists, psychiatrists, psychologists, etc.—has been that punishment is not the answer. Crime, according to these experts, is a very complex phenomenon caused by environmental factors such as poverty, discrimination, unemployment, and so forth. The widespread academic popularity for this point of view is demonstrated by the fact that it appears again and again in federally financed research studies.

"We have had several major studies of the subject [violence]," writes William H. Blanchard, University of Southern California psychologist, "with the government hiring the best professional talent. The answer is always the same. The cause of violence is injustice. But the correction of social injustice means major social change, so we rush off to order another study."[4]

In December, 1969, the National Commission on Violence issued a report on an eighteen-month study based on the research and testimony of more than two hundred leading American scholars. The report said, "The way in which we can make the greatest progress toward reducing violence in America is by taking the action necessary to improve the condition of family and community life for all who live in our cities, and especially the poor who are concentrated in the ghetto slums."[5]

In a recent speech, Judge David L. Bazelon of the United States court of appeals in Washington talked of criminal violence in these terms: "Our existing knowledge suggests that the roots of street crime lie in poverty plus. Plus prejudice, plus poor housing, plus inadequate education, plus insufficient food and medical care…and perhaps more importantly, plus a bad family environment or no family at all."[6]

The problem with the poverty-causes-crime theory is that it does not fit the facts. Crime and violence have risen to new heights in the United States during the same years in which there has been a decline in poverty and vastly increased expenditures for welfare and education. If poverty is the cause of crime, then why has crime in affluent neighborhoods steadily increased?

Arthur Shenfield, British barrister and economist who served as a visiting professor at several American universities, stated emphatically that poverty does not cause crime. He wrote:

"Suppose that a country has no slums and no depressed ghettos. Suppose that it has no significant racial and religious divisions or conflicts. Suppose that adequate quality of housing is available on assisted terms to all. Suppose that the government redistributes income so that no one is in any dire need. Then if popular views about the causes of crime were well founded, such a country would be almost free from crime. At least it would be free from crime such as robbery, burglary, street mugging and the like, although no doubt some crimes, such as those of passion or sexual deviation, might persist.

Sweden is a country with the above-listed conditions. Yet today crime is one of the most striking phenomena of growth in Swedish society. This applies both to crimes of an old-age character, such as robbery, burglary, and street violence, and to newer crimes such as car theft, illegal gambling and bookmaking, dealing in drugs and illicit liquor, and, above all, welfare frauds. So lawless have the cities become that the Stockholm police have been instructed to ignore burglaries in order to concentrate on grave crimes of violence and on those where the suspect is already in custody. Not only is the crime rate high, it is also growing fast.... A further related development of ominous proportions is the rise of juvenile delinquency and, in particular, of acts of vandalism and drug addiction among the young."[7]

LACK OF STANDARDS AS A CAUSE OF CRIME

One can assume that the root cause of crime, violence, drug addiction, and other symptoms of irresponsible behavior is, for the most part, the result of inadequate or inaccurate ethical instruction. Or, put another way, *responsible behavior must be taught.*

The early warnings by educators, law enforcement and others, have not been heeded. In 1981, then Chief Justice Burger, addressing the American Bar Association about what he called a "reign of terror in American cities," said, "We have established a system of criminal justice that provides more protection, more safeguards, more guarantees for those accused of crime than any other nation in all history." In addition, he said, "part of the problem stems from the fact that we have virtually eliminated from the public schools and higher education any effort to teach values."[8]

The idea that irresponsible behavior is caused by inadequate overall education is consistent with the thinking of some of history's greatest students of human behavior. Confucius, for example, in the fifth century B.C., said, "Men possess a moral nature; but if they are well fed, warmly clad, and comfortably lodged without at the same time being instructed, they become like unto beasts."[9]

Dr. John A. Howard, when president of Rockford College and with twenty-five years of experience in college administration, stated emphatically, "The continuing sharp decline among college students in their commitment to the traditional moral values of society...is, in my opinion, the predictable result of the prevailing philosophy of higher education. It is a philosophy which denies any institutional obligation to provide an understanding of our moral heritage, and which proudly protects those who reject that heritage."[10]

One of the most powerful early warning alarms came in *"Amoral America"* the title of a 1975 book by two political scientists, Drs. George C. S. Benson and Thomas S. Engeman. The book is a well-documented study of the relationship between crime and ethical instruction.

"Our astounding crime rate," the authors conclude, "is largely due to lack of ethics, which, in turn, is due to lack of ethical instruction in the schools and other opinion-forming institutions."[11]

The authors continue: "Our thesis is that there is a severe and almost paralyzing ethical problem in this country. Many people dispute this. There are some who do not believe there is a major crime problem; there are some who deny that ethics and crime are related.... We believe that we can demonstrate that unlawful behavior is, in part, a result of absence of instruction in individual ethics. As political scientists, we have not been merely content to trace the course of the decline in ethical instruction and its correlation with increased crime; we are also interested in analyzing methods by which ethics can be encouraged...."

"Contemporary Western society, and especially American society, suffers from inadequate training in individual ethics. Personal honesty and integrity, appreciation of the interests of others, nonviolence and abiding by the law are examples of values insufficiently taught at the present time.... The schools and churches are well situated to teach individual ethical responsibility, but do not do so."[12]

Undoubtedly, scholars, public officials, education and law enforcement officials have, for the past decade and a half, been sounding the alarm. The good news is that those early warnings are finally being heard.

The early 90s have seen a definite swing toward a new way of combating crime, violence and other youthful maladaptive behaviors. Schools are returning to the systematic teaching of common core values. In addition, such community based organizations as the national YMCA and others are creating specific programs that infuse character lessons into their existing programs.

As schools become aware of the need for character education entire communities are also becoming involved. There is a general awareness emerging in small and large communities that forecast a shift toward resolving the problems faced and caused by a minority of youth in our schools and communities.

The question of what is wrong with youth today, is beginning to be replaced by, what can be done to help youth overcome the pressures, influences, mistakes, poor decisions and other factors that impact their lives? The answers seem to relate more to causes than to symptoms.

The question no longer is, should society take seriously the issue of character education as crime prevention, but how and where character education should take place?

RECAP:

1. Over the past 3 plus decades, there has been a shift away from character and values education in the schools and homes.
2. There has been a corresponding increase in various forms of inappropriate youth behavior.
3. More recently, people are recognizing that the solutions to youth problems may rest with the reintroduction of systematic character and values education in our schools, homes and communities.

THE GLOBAL PERSPECTIVE

Civilization is the victory of persuasion over force.

Plato

Since ancient times, wise men have known the crucial importance of ethics and ethical instruction for individuals and society. Aristotle, for example, said, "All who have meditated on the art of governing mankind have been convinced that the fate of empires depends upon the education of youth."

Philosophy professor Andrew Oldenquist says:

> "If we were anthropologists observing members of a tribe, it would be the most natural thing in the world to expect them to teach their morality and culture to their children and, moreover, to think that they had a perfect right to do so on the ground that cultural integrity and perpetuation depend on it.
>
> "Indeed, if we found that they had ceased to teach, through ritual and other organized means, the moral and other values of their culture, we would take them to be on the way to cultural suicide."[1]

Dr. Norman Vincent Peale has been quoted as saying that: "We are living in probably the most undisciplined age in history. Well, if this age is indeed liable to so serious a charge, it should be of interest to know whether the past owed its differing condition to accident or whether this may have been related to specific measures which it has taken. What, in this connection, have other ages done? I suggest that we direct our attention to a few examples of past practice.

First, what about primitive cultures? At adolescence boys are given "moral instruction, including tribal usage relating to obedience, courage, truth, hospitality, sexual relationships, reticence and perseverance.

"Sometimes long periods of silence are imposed upon novices in connection with the puberal ceremonies of most primitive people....Australian boys go alone into the bush, and are required to maintain silence for long periods. African lads are required to remain silent and immobile for long periods. Such practices test a boy's obedience and self-control, and render teachings associated with them especially impressive."

As to education in ancient Egypt, we are told that morals were its (central feature).... Civilization demanded the evolution and enrichment of moral life. To this end the Egyptians sought to train and instruct their young in the art of virtuous living. Their method of moral cultivation was a great advance beyond the simple training of primitive society.... The sage old vizier, Ptah-hotep, in the 27th century B.C. wrote, 'Precious to a man is the virtue of his son, and good character is a thing remembered.' This is said to be the first recorded use of the word 'character' in literature.... The Egyptian use of the word character signified 'to shape, to form, or build.'[2]

EARLY AMERICAN SCHOOLS

Historically, American children have, as previously stated, received far more ethical instruction than children do today. "Traditionally," states Dr. Maurice Connery, dean of the UCLA School of Social

Welfare, "American education at all levels has carried a clear moral mandate, whether it was expressed in the instructions and evaluations given for 'citizenship' in the primary grades, or the more sophisticated moral philosophy of liberal higher education. This emphasis was muted in the swing toward scientific empiricism and the ethical relativity that has dominated our ethical orientation in the last quarter century."[3]

John R. Silber, president of Boston University, and university professor of philosophy and law, provides the following information about early American education:

Long before a child went to school, from seventeenth century to early twentieth-century America, he learned simple verities. And he learned them first, not from teachers of philosophy or ministers of the Gospel, but literally at his mother's knee through such collections as Mother Goose. In Mother Goose we find moral lessons that were thought to be far too important to await the public schools at age six. "If wishes were horses, beggars would ride." This is Mother Goose's reminder to forget about the pleasure principle. Remember the reality principle, the child was told. Don't be misled by the attraction of wishful thinking.

Recently, I read some seventeenth- and eighteenth-century schoolbooks used to teach reading and spelling to young American children, frequently by parents who taught their children at home. These books typically had a rhyme for every letter of the alphabet, for the authors recognized the delight that children take in rhymes. The most famous of these, The New England Primer, *begins:*

A. Adam and Eve their God did grieve.
B. Life to mend this book [the Bible] attend. (And a picture of the Bible was shown.)
C. The cat doth play, and after, slay. (Cats weren't just pets in the 18th and 19th centuries; they were killers; they ate mice, and children were not protected from this grisly information.)

D. Dogs will bite a thief at night. (This is a warning to thieves, if not to dogs.)

F. The idle fool is whipped at school. (And you could add the corollary: the teacher was not sent to prison.)

J. Job felt the rod, yet blessed his God.

Q. Queens and Kings must lie in the dust. (This is a reminder to a child who has not yet gone to school that even kings and queens are mortal.)

T. Time cuts down the great and small. (In case the child was slow and had missed the point in regard to kings and queens, it is mentioned again. Repetition was recognized as conducive to learning.)

X. Xerxes the Great shared the common fate.

Now, does the child get it? That's three times. This was a primer for first reading exercises and this was the way they taught the alphabet. And I submit that by addressing the inevitability of death several times through twenty-six letters of the alphabet, it addresses the child on a far more dignified level than that adopted by the authors of the contemporary Dick and Jane: "Spot and Jane, run and play. Run, Spot, run. Catch, Jane, catch. Dick and Jane are friends." The New England Primer was written in a period before condescension of children had been accepted as a norm for professional educators.

Consider, moreover, how children were taught to write. The art of penmanship, lost some years ago in the United States, was once taught by the use of copybooks, in which beautifully handwritten sentences were presented to the child at the head of the page, and the child was expected to imitate in his own copybook the excellently written headings. And what did the copybook heading say? What were the statements at the top of the page which the child had to copy over and over again, in the process learning them by heart? Let me read from one of the most widely used copybooks of the period.

Persevere in accomplishing a complete education...

That is the heading for a child who has not yet learned how to write. The child was expected to copy it several times. Persevere in accomplishing a complete education. Persevere in accomplishing a complete education. Persevere in accomplishing a complete education. And eventually, a big word like persevere, is learned by heart, and the meaning of perseverance is learned by persevering long enough to write it twenty times. Note the important and exciting use of truly adult words. Children like to imitate their parents; they like to go around in adult clothes, big shoes, and big hats. They also like to imitate adults by using big words. The educators of this period knew the attraction and the power of language. In these copybooks words appear as treasures, language appears as a treasure house, and education as the key. I read some others:

A stitch in time saves nine.
Quarrelsome persons are always dangerous companions.
Employment prevents vice.
An idle mind is the devil's workshop.
Great men were good boys.
Justice is a common right.
Know much, display little.
Wit should never wound.
Build your hopes of fame on virtue.
Zeal for justice is worthy of praise.

These are the efforts of an earlier generation to acquaint their children with various aspects of an undiminished reality, an unreduced reality that is the fusion of facts and values, with reality that is not merely physical, but also moral and spiritual.

Their concern to introduce moral and spiritual content into the education of each child expressed their concern to educate children to the full dimensions of reality—to prepare them, in short, for true human existence. It was not enough merely to talk about mathematics and arithmetic. It was not enough to talk about writing, just as a form of expression, or penmanship as a form of beautiful writing. It was important to have content in the curriculum, and that content was a distillation of a high culture.[4]

EUROPEAN EDUCATION

European educators, according to Benson and Engeman, were exposed to the same intellectual ideas that persuaded American educators gradually to abandon ethical instruction. Freud, Kant, and the existentialists were all Europeans, and Dewey and other American intellectuals were read in Europe.

The influence of these ideas, however, was less in Europe than in the United States. European countries had no First Amendment restriction regarding religion, and Freud and Dewey were not taken as seriously in Europe as in America.

"Perhaps," suggests Engeman, "because the European universities educated a smaller proportion of the population, university students were better selected and less likely to accept new doctrines as enthusiastically as did Americans."[5]

JAPANESE SCHOOLS EMPHASIZE ETHICS

Reed J. Irvine, an authority on Japanese culture, says:

"Traditionally, Oriental education was concerned more with the cultivation of character than with the mastery of skills or the acquisition of useful information. The teacher was valued as a man of high character who could, by precept and example, influence the moral development of his pupils. He was supposed to be a man of learning, but he was even more revered for his character and his exemplary conduct...."

The Japanese educators were influenced by the nineteenth-century English writer Samuel Smiles, whose most famous book, Self-Help, impressively documented the traits of character that had contributed to the great achievements of outstanding statesmen, writers, scientists and artists. Smiles, in turn, had been influenced by Plutarch, whose "Lives" were written to show virtue or vice in men and were used to mold the character of many generations of school boys."

Mr. Irvine says that character instruction was very successful in Japan. "Prewar Japan was poor economically, but the incidence of crime and delinquency was extremely low. It is said that not a single murder was committed in Okinawa, the poorest of all the Japanese prefectures, in the fifty years preceding World War II."[6]

In 1972 Mrs. George Romney, wife of the former Michigan Governor, told a Washington, D.C. audience of her recent visit to Japan. She said that a group of Japanese educators told her that American educational experts who came to Japan after the World War II surrender advised them to eliminate ethical instruction from the public school curriculum. Now, she says, the Japanese educators are convinced that this was bad advice, and they are rapidly moving to reinstate character education."[7]

REDISCOVERING THE AMERICAN ETHIC

America's Founding Fathers were convinced that ethical instruction was essential to maintaining the social system that they had created. Thomas Jefferson often made this point, and Franklin, Madison, Washington, and other early Americans agreed with Jefferson. Said Franklin, "Nothing is more important for the public weal than to form and train up youth in wisdom and virtue."[8]

Most Americans have been taught that the United States was founded on the Judeo-Christian ethic. This is not entirely correct. The American ethic is compatible with Judeo-Christian principles, but it includes ideas about economics, government, law, education, and ethics that were more directly derived from the Founders' study of history and philosophy.

Although their religious viewpoints differed, the Founders believed in a purposeful, rational universe.

Thomas Paine spoke for most of the Founders when he said: "When we survey the work of creation... we see unerring order and universal harmony reigning throughout the whole. No part contradicts another... God is the power of first cause, Nature is the law, and matter is the subject acted upon."[9]

This was the starting point for the American ethic—the idea that the universe was orderly and regulated by rational laws that could be discovered by the study of history, philosophy, religion, and man himself. This basic tenet was stated explicitly in the Declaration of Independence: "When in the course of human events, it becomes necessary for one people to dissolve the political bonds which have connected them with another, and to assume among the powers of the earth, the separate and equal station to which the Laws of Nature and of Nature's God entitle them . . ."[10]

To say that the United States was founded on the Judeo-Christian ethic alone is to ignore the fact that the principles upon which this nation was founded were considered to be universal and applicable to people of all faiths. Walter Kaufmann, Princeton professor of philosophy, has pointed out that the Founders were influenced at least as much by the Greeks and Romans as by the Jews.[11]

Carl L. Becker, distinguished professor of history at Cornell University from 1917 to 1941, wrote:

"Not all Americans... would have accepted the philosophy of the Declaration, just as Jefferson phrased it, without qualification, as the "common sense of the subject"; but one may say that the premises of this philosophy, the underlying preconceptions from which it was derived, were commonly taken for granted. There is a "natural order" of things in the world, cleverly and expertly designed by God for the guidance of mankind, that the "law"

of this natural order may be discovered by human reason; that these laws so discovered furnished a reliable and immutable standard for testing the ideas, the conduct, and the institutions of men—these were the accepted premises, the preconceptions of most eighteenth-century thinking, not only in America, but also in England and France."[12]

The gradual abandonment of the American ethic began more than a hundred years ago. It was then that the approach to human problems began to shift from theologians, philosophers, and historians to the behavioral scientists. Excited by scientific success in solving complex technical problems, scholars set out to use the same scientific methods to solve human problems. The practical lessons of history, philosophy, and religion were, for the most part, ignored—labeled unscientific.

The social and behavioral scientists were not the only ones who gradually abandoned the American ethic and its emphasis on ethical instruction, but they certainly played an influential role. "If the object of education is the improvement of men," wrote Robert M. Hutchins,

"...then any system of education that is without values is a contradiction in terms. A system that seeks bad values is bad. A system that denies the existence of values denies the possibility of education. Relativism, scientism, skepticism, and anti-intellectualism, the Four Horsemen of the philosophical Apocalypse, have produced that chaos in education which will end in the disintegration of the West."[13]

Now, fortunately, there is a small but growing scholarly rediscovery of the American ethic. Few of those involved would describe their ideas in this way. They prefer to think of their work as a rediscovery of ethical principles or individual responsibility or rational man.

Professors Peck and Havighurst, for example, suggest that basic ethical principles may have a scientific basis:

> *"It is just beginning to be conceivable that we may be able to collect some arguable facts about human nature which will, once and for all, demonstrate that the ethical principles held by the Rational Altruists are not just a nice sentiment, but a set of directions for living based on the deepest, most inexorable demands of human nature... Whiting and Child make a similar observation, from the most relevant kind of cross-cultural data, "the confirmation (of our predictions) has been sufficient, we feel, to suggest strongly that there are some principles of personality development which hold true for mankind in general and not just for Western culture."*[14]

The work of the late American psychologist, Dr. Abraham Maslow, is especially significant in this regard. Not only did Maslow, as a *scientist*, recognize the failure of value-free behavioral science, but he also developed a viable, alternative scientific theory—the Third Force—which is compatible with the religion-based American ethic.

"This is not an improvement of something," he wrote about his theory; "it is a real change in direction altogether. It is as if we have been going North and are now going South instead."

Maslow was convinced that the methods of the physical sciences were not suitable for the study of people. He said, "Most of the psychology on this... value-free, value-neutral model of science... is certainly not false but merely trivial... This model which developed from the study of objects and things has been illegitimately used for the study of human beings. It is a terrible technique. It has not worked."[15]

He suggested that the study of human beings should emphasize success and health, the study of the best specimens, rather than the study of neurotic people, rats, pigeons, and statistically average humans.

Another important feature of his approach was his insistence on the acceptance of all sources of knowledge about people. "It is both useful and correct," he wrote, "to consider as falling within the definition of knowledge, all 'protoknowledge' so long as its probability of being correct is greater than chance."[16] This radical (to science) idea reopens the door to the consideration of history, philosophy, and religion.

From a study of healthy human specimens, people he described as "self-actualizers"—Thomas Jefferson, Albert Einstein, Eleanor Roosevelt, Jane Addams, William James, Albert Schweitzer, Abraham Lincoln, and others—Maslow concluded that all humans shared common basic psychological needs. These basic needs are biological in origin, and either unchanging or changing so slowly that for all practical purposes they are unchanging. These needs are weak in the sense that many individuals never discover them, but also strong in that when they are insufficiently met, the result is emotional disturbance, depression, pathology.

"The ultimate disease of our time," said Maslow, "is valuelessness... This state is more crucially dangerous than ever before in history."[17] His research led him to the conclusion that there were enduring ethical principles, as all major religions have claimed, but now one can study these principles using a rational, systematic approach. Maslow, in other words, created a scientific explanation of human behavior that is compatible with the Founding Fathers' theory of natural law. But since the new theory is scientific, it can be taught in public schools and colleges where religious instruction is forbidden.

It seems obvious, from the information presented in this chapter, that many past societies recognized the need to teach their young how to be virtuous. If the reader accepts Jefferson's statement that "virtue is not hereditary," then it also seems obvious that our modern society must place greater emphasis on ethical instruction if we wish to avoid the disintegration of our society.

The bad news is that ethical and character instruction has declined globally. For example, many countries are currently experiencing increases in the same negative behavior that the United States has experienced. Many attribute this breakdown in values to the same factors that has been experienced in America. While it may be instructive to examine the historical and global picture, it is also important to consider that the increase in crime, violence and other anti-social behaviors in America may predate what is occurring internationally.

It appears that the decline in the teaching and practice of ethics and values is becoming a world wide problem.

Recap:

1. Historically, teaching the young to become ethical adults has been the practice of all major civilizations.
2. In many cases, failure to teach the next generation how to be ethical citizens has been a contributing factor in the decline of nations, cultures and governments.
3. The evidence appears to indicate that the need to increase ethical training of the young is an international problem.

IS CHARACTER EDUCATION NEGLECTED?

That moral training is an important part of public school education, no one will deny....And that it receives all the attention its importance demands, few will affirm.

John Swett,
*California Superintendent
of Public Instruction (1863)*

Years ago the distinguished scholar John Ruskin said, "The entire object of education is to make people not merely do the right things, but enjoy the right things: not merely learned, but to love knowledge; not merely pure, but to love purity; not merely just, but to hunger and thirst after justice."

Unfortunately, John Ruskin's concept of the purpose of education appears not to have been in American schools for the past 25-30 years. In recent decades, there has been a steady decline in efforts to systematically teach character in our public schools. This decline, we are convinced, is one major reason for the explosive increase in crime, violence, alcoholism, drug addiction, and other disturbing manifestations of moral decay in our society. If this is so, then one of the most effective and economical ways to reduce these problems is to improve the quantity and quality of ethical instruction in all of our institutions, particularly our public schools.

Looking at character from an historical perspective, there are clear indications that the decline in systematic character education has its roots as far back as the 1960s.

For example, in 1967, Sandrah Pohorlak, University of Southern California scholar, made a comprehensive survey of the status of the teaching of moral and spiritual values in the public schools of the United States. She directed a personal letter and questionnaire to the superintendent or commissioner of education in 55 states, possessions, and territories. The instrument asked, "...how are you treating moral and spiritual values?" Of the agencies queried, all but six replied, and some of them also sent samples of their teaching manuals. The survey revealed that all but eighteen states mentioned moral education among their educational objectives. In spite of this fact, forty-two state departments of education provided nothing in the way of texts, handbooks, or guides to help their teachers teach values; notable exceptions were Florida, Maine, and Alabama.

Mrs. Pohorlak concluded:

> *"Here in America, since 1900 or thereabouts, various forces have resulted in the gradual relinquishment of our original standards for morals and ethics, in education, business, and social relationships.... There is little or no encouragement from the State Offices of Education that the districts they preside over be active in finding ways to improve the teaching and encouragement of moral and spiritual values in their school communities."*[1]

Approximately a year after the Pohorlak study was completed, the California Board of Education released a report entitled "Guidelines for Moral Instruction in California Schools" by Edwin F. Klotz. As Mrs. Pohorlak had done, Dr. Klotz asked the educational leaders in each of the fifty states what they were doing about moral education. He found that only 13 states identified an ongoing program of moral instruction or were in the process of starting one. Four states said they had no committee or guidelines but were interested in what California was doing, and 24 states replied that they had neither guidelines nor a committee studying the problem. Dr. Klotz also surveyed 1,100 California school districts and found that only 40 had guidelines or other prepared materials. Seventy-four districts stated that such materials were under preparation, and 447 districts replied that they integrated such instruction throughout the curriculum, but that the instruction was more incidental than direct. Dr. Klotz concluded:

"The few guides we received from out of state we found to be not as well developed as the "moral and spiritual values guides developed by Ventura and Los Angeles counties.... Most of the guides the California districts submitted were sketchy and did not develop subject matter but usually stated requirements of the law."[2]

Benson and Engeman provide impressive evidence in their book *Amoral America* that emphasis on ethical instruction has declined in all of our institutions—homes, schools, colleges, media, and even in many churches. Professor Benson states:

"Until the First World War, ethics was a required course (in addition to chapel attendance) for undergraduates in private liberal arts colleges of denominational background. The texts for these courses can still be found in college libraries....Although these books vary in their approach to the true ground for ethics—emphasizing first natural law, then passion, then reason—they all share a common concern for improving the character of students."

Dr. Benson cites another study, this time about child rearing:

"It was observed that the change in the articles written on the subject reflected the change in general intellectual attitudes. The percentage of topics dealing with various aspects of character and/

or personality training in three women's magazines was found to be as follows: 1880, 35 percent; 1900, 31 percent; 1910, 39 percent; 1920, 3 percent; 1930, 24 percent; 1940, 23 percent; 1948, 21 percent."[3]

Although interest in child rearing had declined and then increased again, after 1930 the emphasis was quite different. It had shifted from character development to concern with personality. Problems of personal adjustment rather than moral problems were emphasized.

PREVIOUS WARNINGS

Many scholars have warned of the severe dangers of a social system that fails to maintain and communicate its system of values. Until recently these warnings have been generally ignored—and our society, as well as others, continues to deteriorate.

For example, in December 1940, Walter Lippmann spoke to the annual meeting of the American Society for the Advancement of Science. He said:

"During the last forty or fifty years, those who are responsible for education have progressively removed from the curriculum the Western culture which produced the modern democratic state. The schools and colleges have, therefore, been sending out into the world men who no longer understand the creative principles of the society in which they must live.... Prevailing education is destined if it continues, to destroy Western civilization and is in fact destroying it."[4]

There have been repeated warnings along these lines through the 1960s, 70s, 80s and 90s. However, the prevailing response remained one of denial and acquiescence. Schools pointed at parents, parents at schools, and society in general pointed at everyone else.

WHY IS CHARACTER EDUCATION NEGLECTED?

Reasons for the decline in ethical instruction are complex. Concern for the separation of church and state has undoubtedly been an important factor. Dr. Benjamin Wood, when director of the Bureau for Collegiate Educational Research, Columbia University, some years ago referred to the "lamentable disengagement of American education from its indispensable role in the moral-ethical realm." He said that this disengagement

> "arose from a grievously erroneous interpretation of the wise separation of church and state, which error, in turn, grew out of the older and unfortunately still widely accepted error of confusing morality and ethics with one or another specific ecclesiastical affiliation—a basic error which holds that good morals or sound ethics are somehow dependent upon the acceptance of sectarian doctrines and rituals."[5]

The increased complexity of society, and thus of education, has been a factor, as has the demand for greater emphasis on technical knowledge.

Another rationale frequently offered by educators is, if teachers are to succeed in teaching children how to behave, then teachers must receive encouragement and support from the community, parents, legislators, and media. Such support has often been lacking.

Dr. Edwin Klotz, in his study for the California Board of Education, concluded:

> "The schools cannot perform this task [of moral instruction] when beyond the classroom, society is permeated with pictures, films, books, video games and television programs which tend to undermine the very moral structure the schools are by law required to preserve and revere."[6]

Experts may argue about the influence of the media on youthful attitudes, but few deny that there has been a marked change in the quantity and quality of the media message to young people. When children resort to violence and weapons to solve disputes, it seems obvious that they are learning this behavior somewhere. It is doubtful that this learning is taking place in the school or the home. This, of course, leads to the conclusion that the games children play, the films and television they watch and other media presentations have an influence on their problem solving strategies.

If children view frequent acts of violence as a viable solution to resolve conflicts then the probability that they will employ violent solutions in their own lives increases.

Developing character in young people through the teaching learning process is a difficult task and one that requires training, patience, tact, and skill. It is easy to see why, as public education has grown into a huge "mass-production" industry with steadily increasing curricular demands, character instruction has suffered.

In discussing why there is a decline in ethical instruction, an article by Dr. Donald Thomas, Superintendent of Salt Lake City schools, provides this historical perspective:

> *"In the early days, moral education was a major part of the school experience. Ethical principles were extracted from the* Bible, Poor Richard's Almanac, *and the basic documents of our nation. Thus, Jefferson urged that high schools stimulate students' minds to develop their reasoning faculties, enlarge their minds, cultivate their morals, and instill into them the precepts of virtue and order. As for elementary school students, he proposed that they become acquainted with Grecian, Roman, English, and American history, so they would be adequately informed for participation in community life.*
>
> *Today, however, it is not clear that moral education is fashionable in our schools. It may seem that, in our desire to provide everybody with his 'fair share' and we may call this aim social*

*justice—we have neglected to teach the responsibility of giving,
as well as receiving.*"[7]

ETHICAL RELATIVISM

There is another factor that has affected the decline in the systematic teaching of character. The neglect of character education can be tied, to some degree, to the rise in ethical relativism and values clarification. Ethical relativism takes the position that it is inappropriate to teach ethical concepts because such concepts vary from place to place, person to person and time to time. "The objection of the psychologists to the bag of virtues," states one professor, "is there are no such things."[8]

"In the climate of opinion in which we live," writes Professor David E. Trueblood,

"...particularly in colleges and universities, one of the most popular of all positions is that of ethical relativism. The usual argument runs somewhat as follows: There are many different cultures and civilizations in the world. Each of these has its own orthodoxy about human values, but they are in sharp conflict with one another. Hindus think that it is improper to eat meat or to kill a cow, while Westerners produce cows for the single purpose of killing and eating them. Each group thinks its position is right; therefore, moral values are merely relative to a cultural setting; therefore, moral values are purely subjective; therefore, one is exactly as good as another, for all are lodged merely in human minds and have nothing to do with objective reality."[9]

Louis E. Raths is co-author with Merrill Harmin and Sidney Simon of a popular teacher text entitled *Values and Teaching.* "For this writer," states Dr. Raths, "even the idea that we should use all the resources available to us to produce a certain kind of character is repulsive."

*"We believe that each person has to wrest his own values from
the available array... We are concerned with the process of valuing and not the product... The method recommends that no
moral judgment be made by the teacher, or the child would be
robbed of "choice." "... It should be increasingly clear that the
adult does not force his own pet values upon children. What he
does is create conditions that aid children in finding values if
they choose to do so. When operating with the value theory, it
is entirely possible that children will choose not to develop values."*[10]

There is ample evidence that moral values transcend cultural,
religious, race and economic lines. This will be expanded upon further in Chapter 8.

However, to suggest that children may choose "not" to develop
values is to suggest that they will live their lives in some form of
coma. What is important is that children develop values and character traits that make it possible for people to live harmoniously and
at peace. This is especially critical as the world continues to move
toward instantaneous global communication and interaction.

VALUES CLARIFICATION

As an extension of ethical relativism, an approach to ethical instruction that has gained much attention and academic support is called
Values Clarification or *Moral Values Education*. This approach was
initiated in England and the United States in the early 1960s, and
later became influential in Canada.

This method of ethical instruction is significantly different from
those mentioned in the first part of this chapter. Its supporters advocate teaching young people how to choose values but not which
values to choose.

One of the most influential leaders in this movement was Sidney
Simon, School of Education at the University of Massachusetts. Dr.
Simon rejected what he regards as a fundamental error in traditional

approaches to moral education—indoctrination. He sees this as an attempt by adults to impose values upon the young. Indoctrination, he believes, is not only ineffective but highly objectionable because it is based on the traditional principle that there are right and wrong ways of thinking and acting. Professor Simon stated, "None of us has the 'right' set of values to pass on to other people's children."

Dr. Simon's approach, which he called *Values Clarification*, was for a time the most widely used moral values education program in American elementary and secondary schools. He apparently started with the conviction that traditional moral education is irrelevant in today's complex modern world. Dr. Simon writes:

> "The children of today are confronted by many more choices than in previous generations.
>
> "Areas of confusion and conflict abound: politics, religion, love and sex, family, friends, drugs, materialism, race, work, aging and death, leisure time, school, and health. Each area demands decisions that yesterday's children were rarely called upon to make."

Values Clarification is concerned not with *which* values people develop but *how* they develop their values. The approach seeks to promote growth, freedom, and ethical maturity. The program asks parents, teachers, and other adults to start with the recognition that "there's no right or wrong answer to any question of value."

Teachers are provided with classroom problems or dilemmas that are designed to help students discover their own values. In a typical exercise, the student is asked to answer questions such as:

1. Which do you think is the most religious thing to do on a Sunday morning?
   a. Go to church and hear a very good preacher.
   b. Listen to some classical music on the radio.
   c. Have a big breakfast with the family.

2. Which do you like the least?
   a. An uptight indoctrination.
   b. A cynical debunker.
   c. A dull, boring fact giver.

In another exercise, Simon requests parents and teachers to pose the following problem:

Your husband or wife is a very attractive person. Your best friend is very attracted to him or her. How would you want them to behave?

   a. Maintain a clandestine relationship ' ' you wouldn't know about it.
   b. Be honest and accept the reality of the relationship
   c. *Proceed with a divorce.*[11]

Critics of Values Clarification point out that the traditional response, "behave themselves," isn't even offered as an option.

"Values-clarification 'strategies,'" write Professors Bennett and Delattre,

> *"...are supposed to give students the greatest possible freedom of choice and knowledge of themselves and the world. By accepting the idea that there are no right or wrong answers to questions of morality and conduct, students learn that being clear about what one wants is all that is required to live well. But do such strategies really provide knowledge about the world and freedom of choice? Do they actually make for self-knowledge and ethical maturity and autonomy?... The first exercise, about the most religious thing to do on a Sunday morning, asks the student to think about what he wants and likes to do on Sunday mornings. Yet it introduces no other considerations, and implies that whatever the student thinks is religious, thereby is religious.."*[12]

COGNITIVE MORAL DEVELOPMENT

The psychologist, Lawrence Kohlberg founded the Center for Moral Development at Harvard University. He, like Simon, was highly critical of traditional moral education, viewing it as useless and totalitarian. He too has "objected to the deliberate effort to inculcate majority values... as a violation of the child's moral freedom." Dr. Kohlberg, however, believes that Simon's approach is too relativistic and leads students to the conclusion that ethical relativity is true. Kohlberg believes the relativism is scientifically incorrect.

Kohlberg calls his method *Cognitive Moral Development* and emphasizes the need for a sound theory on the development of moral reasoning. He traces his ideas to John Dewey and Jean Piaget and states that people's thinking about moral problems develops through specific stages. These stages of moral development are invariable and occur regardless of race or culture.

Kohlberg's six stages, briefly outlined, are:

Stage 1.   Action is motivated by avoidance of punishment, and "conscience" is a non-rational fear of punishment.

Stage 2.   Action is motivated by desire for reward or benefit. Possible guilt reactions are ignored and punishment viewed in a pragmatic manner.

Stage 3.   Action is motivated by anticipation of disapproval of others, actual or imagined hypothetical.

Stage 4.   Action is motivated by anticipation of dishonor, that is, institutionalized blame for failure of duty, and by guilt over concrete harm done to others.

Stage 5.   Action is motivated by concern about maintaining respect of equals and of the community (assuming their respect is based on reason rather than emotions). Concern about own self-respect, that is, to avoid judging self as irrational, inconsistent, non-purposeful.

Stage 6. Action is motivated by concern about self-condem-
nation for violating one's own principles. (Differentiates between community respect and self-respect.)
Differentiates between self-respect for generally
achieving rationality and self-respect for maintaining
moral principles.[13]

Kohlberg emphasizes the child's right to freedom of choice. He
postulated that there is one universal, all-inclusive ethical principle—
justice. People can be helped to move to higher stages of moral
development, but less than twenty percent of all adults ever develop
beyond Stage 4.

Professor Kohlberg's typical classroom exercise is the moral di-
lemma. Dilemmas are intended to stimulate student discussion and
enable students to move to higher stages of moral development.

A book listing some dilemmas, hypothetical dilemmas for use
in moral discussions, has been prepared and is distributed by the
Center for Moral Development. Here is a typical excerpt from this
book:

"SWAPPING "

A number of married couples who knew each other were
thinking of "swapping" (changing partners for sexual inter-
course). The couples lived in the same neighborhood and
knew each other quite well. They were people in their late
thirties or early forties. They felt that they would like to have
new sexual experiences. They felt that after being married
for so long and having sex with the same person, sex had
become quite dull.

1. If all the couples agreed to it, would it be all right for them
to change partners? Why or why not.

2. Recently there have been a number of "swapping" cases re-ported in the   newspapers. The public's general reaction is very negative. Why do you think people react this way? Do you agree or disagree with them? Give your reasons.
3. If the couples had children, would this make any difference? What effect do you think "swapping" would have on the children?
4. What could some of the possible positive effects be?
5. What could some of the possible negative effects be?

Of the fifty dilemmas listed in the book, twenty-one are related to sexual conflicts—homosexuality, swapping, extramarital sex, etc. Other dilemmas mention My Lai, Daniel Barrigan, Daniel Ellsberg, women's liberation, kidney transplants, draft evasion, and abortion.

Professor Kohlberg makes the following comments about the use of dilemmas:

> *"It is not always necessary that the matters discussed be ones of the immediate and real-life issues of the classroom. I have found that my hypothetical and remote, but obviously morally real and challenging conflict, situations are of intense interest to almost all adolescents and lead to lengthy debate among them. They are involving, because the adult right answer is not obviously at hand to discourage the child's own moral thought, as so often is the case."*[14]

It is interesting to reflect upon this notion. Professor Kohlberg obviously has faith that adolescents have sufficiently mature ethical reasoning powers to make choices that are moral. While it is true that the process (debates) may be valuable, the absence of any di-rection as to the morality of a decision leaves this process lacking.

DO THE VALUES CLARIFICATION
APPROACHES WORK?

Professor Kohlberg, and his colleagues, such as Raths Harmin and Simon, who wrote *Values and Teaching*, have had great impact on professional educators. However, their methods have also aroused a great deal of controversy.

One might ask, are young people capable of developing a sound code of ethics without exposure to the ideas of the great philosophers and the accumulated wisdom of the ages? There are those who believe that exposure to great ideas as one element of character development leads to contempt for authority and tradition. While there is no evidence to support this point of view it has had a negative effect upon attempts to teach values through literature.

Parent groups in several communities have been highly critical of Values Clarification and opposed its use in public schools. Richard A. Baer, Jr., Cornell University professor, provides the following information about opposition to Values Clarification:

> "Back in the mid-1960s, social scientists Louis E. Raths, Merrill Harmin, and Sidney B. Simon developed the teaching method known as Values Clarification, advertising it as an ideal way to deal with values without taking sides or indoctrinating students in one particular value position...
>
> "Parents did not react immediately. But when children began to report over dinner that class discussion had been about whether lying was sometimes permissible and whether they should always obey their parents, it wasn't long before groups of parents began to mobilize against Values Clarification.
>
> "Many of these parents were Christian fundamentalists. Their arguments were not couched in the sophisticated jargon of philosophy or social science, and sometimes emotions outstripped logic. But they left little doubt that they thought

Values Clarification was teaching their children a kind of ethical relativism.

"Instead of meeting such objections with solid arguments of their own, many educators attacked the objectors, dismissing their criticism as little more than a reactionary fundamentalist response to education innovation.... Over the past seven years, non-fundamentalist scholars from major universities—including Professors Kenneth A. Strike of Cornell, Alan L. Lockwood of the University of Wisconsin, and John S. Stewart, formerly of Michigan State University—have faulted Values Clarification on at least a dozen counts. The list of critics also includes William J. Bennett...and Edwin J. Delattre, president of St. John's College in Annapolis. The major objections of these writers are virtually identical with those initially raised by religious fundamentalists and other parents groups.

"First, contrary to what its proponents claim, Values Clarification is not values. Even on the level of particular ethical decisions, where the authors try hard to be neutral, they succeed only partially. As Messrs. Bennett and Delattre point out, the approach used in such Values Clarification strategies as Sidney Simon's 'Priorities' "emphatically indoctrinates—by encouraging and even exhorting the student to narcissistic self-gratification."

"And on the deeper level of what philosophers call 'metaethics' that is, critical analysis and theory about the nature of values as such—the claim to neutrality is entirely misleading. At this more basic level, the originators of Values Clarification simply assume that their own subjectivist theory of values is correct. By affirming the complete relativity of all values, they, in effect, equate values with personal tastes and preferences. If parents object to their children using pot or engaging in premarital sex, the theory behind Values Clarification makes it appropriate for the child to respond, 'But that's just your value judgment. Don't force it on me.'

"Furthermore, Values Clarification indoctrinates students in ethical relativism, for its proponents push their own position on their captive student audiences and never suggest that thoughtful people may choose alternatives. Sidney Simon, Howard Kirschenbaum, and other Values Clarification authors repeatedly belittle teachers of traditional values. Such teachers, they claim, 'moralize,' 'preach,' 'manipulate,' and 'whip the child into line.' Their positions are 'rigid' and they rely on "religion and other cultural truisms.'

"The second major fault, according to the University of Wisconsin's Alan Lockwood, is that 'a substantial proportion of the content and methods of Values Clarification constitutes a threat to the privacy rights of students and their families.' To be sure, the method permits students to say 'I pass' when the teacher asks them to complete such open-ended sentences as 'If I had 24 hours to live...,' 'Secretly I wish ..,' 'or "My parents are usually ...,' but many of these 'projective techniques are designed in such a fashion, Mr. Lockwood claims, that students often will realize too late that they have divulged more about themselves and their families than they wish or feel is appropriate in a public setting. Moreover, the method itself incorporates pressure toward self-disclosure.

"A third criticism of Values Clarification is that by presupposing very specific views about human nature and society, it becomes a kind of 'religious' position in its own right which competes directly with other religious views."[15]

Reo M. Christenson, professor of political science at Miami University in Oxford, Ohio, is another outspoken critic of Values Clarification. He writes:

"Let me be blunt: Given their meager life experience, their myopic vision and necessarily immature judgment, teenagers lack the ability to formulate independently a sound value system. It is foolish and naive to expect them to. Too many students during these sessions will try to rationalize values that promote their freedom to do as they please."

"Students need to know and have a right to know what thoughtful and responsible people over the centuries have learned about living. If we fail to tell them, we do them a profound disservice."[16]

Lickona, in *Educating for Character*, states: "At best, values clarification raised some important issues for students to think about and encouraged them to close the gap between a value they professed (e.g., 'Pollution is bad') and personal action ('What are you going to do about it?') At its worst, however, values clarification mixed up trivial questions ('Do you like to read the comics?') with important ethical issues ('Should capital punishment be abolished?'). More seriously, it took shallow moral relativism loose in the land and brought it into the schools."

He further concludes that, "In the end, values clarification made the mistake of treating kids like grown-ups who only needed to clarify values that were already sound."[17]

The Values Clarification approaches are still being used in education and have remained controversial. Some educators believe that they are the *best* way to help young people, whereas others believe these approaches are unproductive or actually counterproductive. The authors of this book tend to agree with the latter viewpoint.

It has been said that youth cannot heed a message they have not heard. If the message they receive through values clarification exercises is one of youthful self fulfillment, do my own thing or let's party, then youth will develop a value system based on these messages. We believe that accumulated wisdom of the ages and life experiences provide adults with the rights and responsibility to be more directive in assisting youth in their formation of ethical core values.

Needed to resolve this dispute are careful research studies that concentrate on results obtained by the various approaches to ethical instruction. Extended research should concentrate on desirable outcomes such as reduced vandalism and improved attendance, scholarship, and student behavior.

Recap:

1. Systematic character education began to decline in the schools during the 1960s and 70s.
2. The influence of the media and the rise of the philosophy of ethical relativism had a major impact upon the teaching of ethics, character and values at all levels of the educational spectrum.
3. Ethical relativism also harmfully influenced child rearing which also impacted the school.
4. Previous warnings, dire predictions and observable increases in maladaptive behavior did not foster a change in educational policies regarding character education.

THE SEPARATION OF CHURCH AND STATE

"Without a moral and spiritual awakening there is no hope for us."

Dwight D. Eisenhower

There is prominent objection to the idea that public schools should place greater emphasis on character development; the belief that ethical principles cannot, or at least should not, be taught separately from religion.

Several years ago, the Jefferson Center for Character Education was interviewing candidates to write copy for one of the Center's character-building programs. The job was offered to the applicant who seemed best qualified. However, he declined, and stated that the assignment was in conflict with his religious convictions as a Roman Catholic.

Several weeks later, the applicant called and said that he had discussed this conflict with several of his former professors at Loyola University in Los Angeles. They had informed him that the Roman Catholic church had no objection to character education separate from religion, provided that the principles taught were compatible. They pointed out that Confucianism was a moral philosophy rather than a religion, and that it was perfectly proper for an individual to be both Catholic and Confucian.

The Loyola professors went on to tell the applicant that just after the end of World War II, General Chiang Kai-shek asked some

Catholic scholars to help develop a program to teach moral principles in Chinese schools. He wanted a program that was compatible with all of the various religions represented in China. The Catholic scholars assured him that it was quite feasible to develop an ethical education program based on reason and logic rather than on divine revelation. (Unfortunately, this effort was cut short by the communist takeover in China.)

Many Americans believe that the Supreme Court has ruled against ethical instruction in public schools. This is not true. The First Amendment to the U.S. Constitution states, "Congress shall make no law respecting an establishment of religion, or prohibiting the free exercise thereof."

Much of the misunderstanding of the Supreme Court's position stems from the 1963 *Abington School District v. Schempp* decision by the Court. This decision did not forbid teaching moral or spiritual values or even teaching *about* the Bible. What was found unconstitutional under the "establishment of religion" clause was a Baltimore School Board statute requiring reading from the Bible without comment at the opening of each school day and the recitation of the Lord's Prayer by the students in unison. The Court decided, eight to one, that such school exercises violate the First Amendment.

William J. Brennan, Jr., one of the concurring judges, wrote:

"The holding of the Court today plainly does not foreclose teaching about the Holy Scriptures or about the differences between religious sects in classes of literature or history. Indeed, whether or not the Bible is involved, it would be impossible to teach meaningfully many subjects in the social sciences or the humanities without some mention of religion. To what extent, and at what points in the curriculum religious material should be cited, are matters which the courts ought to entrust very largely to the experienced officials who superintend our nation's public schools. They are experts in such matters, and we are not."[1]

The following statement of policy and position on religion in public education was jointly adopted in 1967 by the Synagogue Council of America and the National Community Relations Advisory Council. It represents a position designed to meet the Supreme Courts standards:

"Insofar as the teaching of spiritual values may be understood to signify religious teaching, this must remain, as it has been, the responsibility of the home, the church, and the synagogue. Insofar as it is understood to signify the teaching of morality, ethics, and good citizenship, a deep commitment to such values has been successfully inculcated by our public schools in successive generations of Americans. The public schools must continue to share responsibility for fostering our commitment to these moral values, without presenting or teaching any sectarian or theological sources or sanctions for such values."[2]

In *Pierce v. Society of Sisters,* the Supreme Court considered the rights and responsibilities of parents and schools in educating children. The Court found that parents had the right to "direct the upbringing and education of children under their control." This, in effect, ensured the right of parents to send their children to the school of their choice.

In addition to affirming the right of parents to select the school of their choice, however, the Court went on to state:

"No question is raised concerning the power of the state reasonably to regulate all schools, to inspect, supervise and examine them, their teachers and pupils, to require that all children of proper age attend some school, that teachers shall be of good moral character and patriotic disposition, that certain studies plainly essential to good citizenship must be taught, and that nothing be taught which is manifestly inimical to the public welfare."[3]

Another relevant precedent is the famous Northwest Ordinance, enacted in 1787. It was approved by the same Congress that wrote and approved the U.S. Constitution, and it was much the same group that passed the First Amendment to the Constitution four years later.

The Ordinance; stated: "Religion, morality, and knowledge being necessary to good government and the happiness of mankind, schools and the means of education shall forever be encouraged."[4]

Although the Constitution itself does not refer to ethical instruction, there are many references to the importance of ethics in the writings by the architects of the Constitution. Thomas Jefferson said, "Virtue is not hereditary"; and, "I know of no safe repository for the ultimate powers of society but the people themselves; and if we think them not enlightened enough to exercise their control with a wholesome direction, the remedy is not to take it from them, but to increase their discretion by education."[5]

Madison said, "To suppose that any form of government will secure liberty or happiness without any virtue in the people, is a chimerical idea."[6]

"I thank God," said Samuel Adams, "that I have lived to see my country independent and free. She may enjoy her independence and freedom if she will. It depends on her virtue."[7]

Franklin was equally vehement. "Only a virtuous people are capable of freedom. As nations become corrupt and vicious, they have more need of masters... Nothing is of more importance for the public weal, than to form and train up youth in wisdom and virtue."[8]

Several years ago, the Maryland General Assembly passed a resolution instructing the governor to appoint a commission to

> "identify and assess ongoing programs in morals and value education in the schools of Maryland, if any, and to make recommendations toward the implementation of these programs into the curriculum."[9]

The commission asked the State Attorney General for a legal opinion on whether there were any legal impediments to the teaching of ethical values in public schools. In July 1979, the commission received a seven-page opinion from Attorney General Stephen H. Sachs, who stated in part:

> *"We have concluded that the fact that ethical values are taught in the public school system does not, standing alone, violate the Establishment and Free Exercise Clauses of the First Amendment of the United States Constitution or any privacy rights arising under the First Amendment... Religion certainly cannot be construed to envelop an educational program that attempts merely to impart basic ethical and moral values to the children of this society."* [10]

THERE MUST BE A CLEAR SEPARATION

There should be no doubt that the inclusion of religious indoctrination with the teaching of character education in the public schools is not only illegal but unethical as well. In establishing a program to systematically teach school children the values of honesty, integrity, respect for law, and the other enduring cross-cultural and universal values, there is always the possibility that someone, somewhere, will breach the gap that separates the teaching of religion from the teaching of character.

The occasional person who chooses to indoctrinate students, however, will probably find subversive ways to carry on this pursuit whether the curriculum is one of character education, social studies, or some other curricular offering.

That a few educators violate the principle of separation of church and state should not be cause for abandoning the teaching of ethical values. Daniel Callahan and Sissela Bok, in their study of the teaching of ethics at the university level, state:

"It would be wholly out of place for university teachers to indoctrinate students with their own moral values or theories, and in particular, to do so in a way that precludes exposure to other moral perspectives. But to let anxiety over the possibility of indoctrination dictate an omission of courses in ethics strikes us as equally odd. While there is always such a risk in higher education—in economics, politics, or law, for example—it is no greater in courses on ethics. Teaching approaches that are reprehensible in other fields are no less so in ethics courses. If one believes, as we do, that enabling students to reach their own moral augments is an important goal of ethics teaching, then the chances of indoctrination are reduced from the start. Faculty should be free to express their viewpoints; failure to do so could represent a special kind of moral bankruptcy. But they have a fundamental obligation to make certain students understand that there are different moral viewpoints—and to help them develop the skills necessary to analyze the teacher's moral values as well as other moral positions."[11]

A careful definition of what values will be included in a character education program can lessen the anxiety and bring a degree of understanding and perhaps resolution to the debate concerning the implementation of character education.

"Our task," said Former Secretary of Education Terrel H. Bell, "is to consider ways of deliberately, systematically, and effectively carrying out moral education in the schools—and to do this in a way that violates none of the ethnic, racial, or religious differences that characterize our country's children."[12]

ETHICAL INSTRUCTION IS REQUIRED IN SOME STATES

In the preceding pages we have described legal decisions to show that character education in public schools is legal. The fact is, character education is not only legal, but required by law in many states.

For example, Section 44806 of the California Education Code reads:

Training of Pupils in Morality and Citizenship
Each teacher shall endeavor to impress upon the minds of the pupils the principles of morality, truth, justice, patriotism, and a true comprehension of the rights, duties, and dignity of American citizenship, including kindness toward domestic pets and the humane treatment of living creatures, to teach them to avoid idleness, profanity, and falsehood, and to instruct them in manners and morals and principles of a free government.[13]

In Michigan the State Board of Education adopted a resolution (March 13, 1968) that stated in part:

RESOLVED, that the State Board of Education urges educators in the schools of Michigan to continue to improve their efforts to foster thoughtful and critical examination of moral values by students and to provide them with the opportunity to practice and demonstrate these values both in the classroom and in extracurricular activities of school, and in their everyday life, so that each student can improve the quality of his own life and of society as a whole. Included in the values which should be particularly developed are self-respect, respect for others, respect for the law, and good citizenship.[14]

Michigan and California are not alone in stressing the need for ethical instruction through the public school system. For example, the North Dakota State Code of Education says:

15-38-10. MORAL INSTRUCTION. Moral instruction tending to impress upon the minds of pupils the importance of truthfulness, temperance, purity, public spirit, patriotism, international peace, respect for honest labor, obedience to parents, and deference to old age, shall be given by each teacher in the public school.[15]

These examples are not exhaustive. Many other states have begun to mandate the systematic teaching of moral principles and values. Some have begun to refer to such practices as character education. In 1995, Alabama mandated the teaching of character education in all schools for a minimum of ten minutes each day. Other states such as Tennessee, Hawaii, Virginia and New Mexico are currently mandating values and character education.

It is important to note that many states are not creating new mandates. They are, in fact, updating or reemphasizing what is already law.

These examples and others not mentioned indicate a trend toward the re-establishment of character education as an integral part of the total curriculum.

WHOSE VALUES OR WHAT VALUES

In working with schools, school districts, communities or, for that matter, states, the question of separation of church and state is often brought forward as an issue. Generally, the question will be couched in terms related to; *Whose* values will you teach? The assumption underlying this question is that people of different religions, ethnic, racial, gender, age or economic groups have nothing in common. This implies the belief that such groups have a set of values separate and apart from other groups. As a result there is no common ground.

In reality, the question; Whose values will you teach? is really the wrong question. A more appropriate question would be, *What* values will you teach?

When the question deals with "whose values" or character traits then there is the fear among some, that there will be an imposition of a particular intrusive set of values.

When the issue is related to "what" values; the concerns related to the imposition of a particular value system can be decreased, if not eliminated.

In schools the answer to the question what values will be taught must take into consideration the four strands that are included in the fabric of personal and social value systems. These four stands, or elements of values or character education, will be discussed more fully in Chapter 6.

Recap:

1. In the minds of some, the paramount question affecting (impediment) character education in public schools has been that of the separation of Church and State.

2. Court decisions have made it clear that character, values and moral education do not violate the principle of the separation of Church and State.

3. Many states have, during the recent past, instituted or re-established the mandate to teach values and character as a part of the school curriculum.

4. A more significant question should be "what" values will be taught, not "whose" values.

FACTORS INFLUENCING CHARACTER EDUCATION

"All who have meditated on the art of governing mankind have been convinced that the fate of empires depends upon the education of youth."

Aristotle

Most people believe that the family has primary responsibility for developing ethical behavior in the young. Unfortunately, it is not nearly as well accepted that in America schools also played a critical role in teaching ethics before 1900. In addition to the home and the school, the religious community, other community organizations, youth and recreational clubs and the media also play a role in instilling values.

Conversely, the lack of positive modeling of values within the community also conveys a message to youth that is counter-productive to developing good character. Members of the community, or organizations within the community who practice unethical behavior, foster the thinking that, "if they can do it so can I."

SOURCES OF DELINQUENCY

Several major studies have emphasized the connection between values and delinquency.

Several years ago the Rampart Division of the Los Angeles Police Department made a study of youth gang violence and vandalism.

The Rampart Division is in a neighborhood in West Central Los Angeles; a densely populated, cosmopolitan inner-city area of diverse economic backgrounds. Approximately 10 criminally involved gangs operated in the Rampart area at the time of the study. The study concluded that lack of discipline within the family structure of many gang-prone youths, and a general lack of discipline in community life as a whole, significantly contributed to the criminal youth gang problem. "One obvious answer," the report states, "is to attempt to instill a socially acceptable sense of values in these youths before they reach adolescence." The report went on to state:

"Normally and ideally, this should be accomplished in the family home, but this is often impossible for a variety of reasons, not the least of which is the inadequacy of some parents.

One of the more practical alternatives for developing citizenship (law and order) values in our youth is through the public school system, for that is the system which traditionally responds to the educational needs of our society. It is there that the public school teacher has prolonged contact with the socially disadvantaged student and is in a position to effectively compensate for some of the inadequacies of parental supervision."[1]

A relevant study was conducted by a distinguished team of Harvard criminologists, Drs. Sheldon and Eleanor Glueck. They examined the lives of more than two thousand delinquents over a period of many years. Their findings are at serious odds with prevailing sociological theories, which place much of the blame for delinquency on poverty and discrimination.

"American criminologists," wrote the Gluecks, "in their preoccupation with sociocultural 'causes' of delinquency and crime, have tended to overlook or minimize the crucial fact that such influences are selective."[2] The Gluecks found that only a small proportion, perhaps 5 to 15 percent, of boys reared in underprivileged areas became delinquents. "Poverty by itself doesn't make a delinquent... You can find low standards of behavior and neglected children in well-to-do families."[3]

The Gluecks discovered a significant difference between homes of delinquent and non-delinquent children in poor neighborhoods. There were many more criminals and drunkards among the fathers of delinquents. The disciplinary methods of both parents were far less adequate than those in the homes of non-delinquents, and delinquents more often came from broken homes.

"What is really required," they stated, "is great firmness administered with love... Love is the essential element... Clearly we must not neglect the fact that it is the emotional poverty, the spiritual poverty, as well as the actual physical poverty that must be recognized."[4]

More recently, Richard H. Blum, an American psychologist, wrote *Horatio Alger's Children*. Blum also related his work to the theme of traditional values or morality. His book examined the role of the family in the origin and prevention of drug risk. The book describes the work of a research team headed by Dr. Blum which made a three-year study of almost a thousand middle-class parents and children. The researchers conclude that children of permissive parents have a far greater chance of becoming hooked on hard drugs than those whose parents are strict but affectionate. Blum writes:

> *"As scientists we were surprised to find that the best protection a child can have against drugs is the old fashioned group of moral virtues.*
>
> *Families that believe in God and country, went to church regularly, loved their children but disciplined them strictly and respected the police were not bothered with a drug problem.*
>
> *But families that believed children must be free to "find themselves," that practiced no religion or very little, and that mistrusted or were disrespectful to authority generally had youngsters who took to drugs."*[5]

As stated earlier, the results of the "do my own thing" morally relativistic parenting can, and often does, produce an adult who does not have a moral compass.

THE CHANGING AMERICAN FAMILY

It seems obvious that many families today are significantly different from the families of forty or fifty years ago. This difference has had a profound effect on the teaching of basic values to children.

Generally, a child born into a pre-World War II family could look forward to a fairly stable environment; with parents who molded the child's character through interpersonal relationships. There would be a mother and father, and they would be the same two people through the childhood and adolescence of the child. And there would probably be four grandparents, several aunts, uncles, cousins, and a number of brothers and sisters. For the most part, this was the rule rather than the exception. A relatively small number of divorces took place—unlike current trends, which indicate a divorce rate of over 50 percent of all marriages.

In addition to this family constellation, there would be a relatively small number of persons who had influential contact with the child during the formative years: a handful of teachers; a priest, minister, or rabbi; local merchants; neighbors; and, of course, the peer group.

All in all, the number of persons important during a youth's early and teen years probably did not exceed thirty people. Additionally, this small number of persons was likely to be fairly homogeneous— that is, because they spent time together, lived and worked near each other, and went to neighborhood schools, they generally held similar beliefs.

There were other influences on children apart from this circle, such as movies, comics, radio, theater, newspapers, books, and magazines. However, by and large, the pre-World War II child had a close group of people who influenced character development.

Children were not bombarded by an extensive array of conflicting models from other persons or sources.

Following World War II, significant changes began to occur in and around the American family. The war took families from the farms and put them into the large industrial cities of the nation. A nation that was once fairly immobile became highly mobile, and with this mobility came a subtle but significant change in the family. Families once living in close proximity found themselves spread all over the continent.

With this mobility also came the growth of the tract home and the moving together of people with diverse ethnic, religious, and personal backgrounds.

As mobility increased, new pressures were placed on the family. Women who had to work during the war effort continued to work; the number of mothers in the work force steadily increased through the late 1940s into the 1950s and has continued into the 1990s. This further changed the structure of the family and introduced children to a variety of persons who took care of them while their parents were at work.

Gradually, it became obvious that the baby boom and the accelerated divorce rate were beginning to have an effect on the American family: Baby boom brought on new pressures; and the divorce rate resulted in a shift in the makeup of the family and the influence parents exerted over children's character development.

These changes have greatly altered the structure of the family and its ability to transmit ethical standards to the next generation.

CHANGING CONCEPTS OF CHILD REARING

In addition to the formidable changes in the makeup of the family, concepts of child rearing shifted. The same intellectual theories that influenced formal education also influenced many parents. Parents, like schools, became more permissive, and emphasis shifted from individual responsibility to a victim mentality—a don't-blame-me point of view. Someone or something else made me do it.

The idea that crime and violence were the fruit of forces outside the individual—poverty, lack of education, etc.—led to a decrease in the emphasis on teaching personal responsibility to their children. The forces that caused crime were thought to be beyond the control of parents, and thus not their responsibility.

Paul Roazen, an authority on Freud, stated that in child rearing, "There was a time in the history of psycho-analytical doctrine when the inclination was to view all suppression as negative, all controls of the child as hindrances to his development."[6]

Richard Blum, whose work we have mentioned, found that low-risk parents, with drug free children, were confident leaders and their children seemed to have strong leadership qualities. High-risk parents, influenced by modern value-free behavioral theories, opposed strong leadership. Dr. Blum says:

"If there is no final authority, if all things are relative, and if man's mind is the highest form of life, the ultimate responsibility of the individual as well as anguish are the results. High-risk parents have accepted, as their ethic, the most spectacularly successful enterprise of this century—the positivistic, pragmatic, scientific model... If parents are not buttressed by traditional moral standards based on a faith in the order of things, they can only rely—insofar as they might wish to counter such hedonism at all—on arguments drawn from a new faith in pragmatism and science."[7]

Dr. Blum and his colleagues discovered not only that children raised to respect traditional values were less apt to suffer from drug abuse problems but also that they and their families were happier. Happiness and pleasure within the family circle were characteristic of low-risk families—pain and humiliation were more typical in high-risk families. "Youth who suffer no drug risk," writes Dr. Blum, "have discovered that the values worth living by are self-respect and respect for others and kindness and responsibility to the family and to oneself."[8]

ORGANIZED RELIGION AND CHARACTER

Organized religion, most people will agree, has played an important part in influencing ethical conduct.

Russell Hill, a retired business executive, studied the ethical concepts of major world religions and concluded that there was general agreement on such ethical concepts as: courage, conviction, generosity, kindness, helpfulness, honesty, justice, tolerance, sound use of time and talents, freedom, and good citizenship.

Several studies of religion in America have shown that a high percentage of Americans are religious. One Gallup poll, for example, estimated that 94 percent of adult Americans believe in God.[9]

Unfortunately, as Benson and Engeman found in their study of religious school curricula, many churches have significantly reduced their former emphasis on individual ethics. Professor Engeman writes:

"The modern church... has, to a large extent, modified its concern with individual ethics. Judeo-Christian ethics has been replaced in the churches' interest by social action and psychological views of individual happiness. In so doing, the churches have followed the intellectual theories coming from the society around them—particularly from the universities. According to these views, individual unhappiness and criminality are consequences of social forces, and are not questions of spiritual or ethical choice. As long as there is racism, militarism, economic exploitation, etc., one should not be surprised—the argument goes—to find criminal reactions to these conditions....

Freud and other psychologists have... had a powerful influence on church men. If criminals are created by early childhood experience or other environmental influences, then it is superfluous to talk about ethical standards and individual responsibility."[10]

Dr. Engeman says that in spite of a large number of studies, the results are inconclusive as to whether religious conviction does modify delinquent behavior. He quotes a 1961 study by Travers and Davis summarizing the existing studies as follows: "Findings are in complete conflict and range from those investigators who view religion as a cure to those who seem to view it as a cause."[11]

It is important to note that the authors' recent experience with groups of teachers in different religious schools has clearly indicated that the various world religions do have a common set of core values.

Work with Muslim, 7th Day Adventist, Lutheran, and Jewish and Roman Catholic educators all resulted in the generation of a list of values that were overlapping. All groups listed such values as honesty, respect, courage, perseverance, responsibility and caring as common values that must be taught in their schools.

It is also true that during the recent past the ability of the faith community to influence the acquisition of values by youth was impaired by at least two factors. The first was the decline in youth participation in religious activities. The second was the reality that youth participation in many religiously sponsored activities e.g.; dances and field trips, was negatively impacted by the increasing cost of insurance. In many cases, extreme increases in insurance rates resulted in decisions that meant various character building activities could no longer take place under church sponsorship.

THE INFLUENCE OF THE MEDIA

It is reasonable to assume that the changes in the family brought about by permissive child-rearing practices, mobility, divorce, and the influence of relativistic science would not have had such a great impact were it not for the power of the media. Once it was reasonable to think of a child thirty or fifty years ago as being shaped by twenty to thirty influential persons. Now it is plausible to consider that thirty to fifty different people, with a wide range of ethical points of view, influence a child each day through television, music and video games.

It would be inaccurate to label television the sole "cause" of the disturbing growth of crime and violence in American society. Nevertheless, it would be irresponsible to overlook the influence of television on the American family as a powerful factor in the character development of young children and the lessening of parents' power to influence that development.

Supporting this point of view, Frederick Wertham, consulting psychiatrist at Queens General Hospital in New York, states in his article, "School for Violence, Mayhem in the Mass Media":

"If somebody had said a generation ago that a school to teach the art and uses of violence would be established, no one would have believed him. He would have been told that those whose mandate is the mental welfare of children, the parents and the professionals, would prevent it. And yet this education for violence is precisely what has happened and is still happening; we teach violence to young people to an extent that has never been known before in history."[12]

He then cites an example:

"Recently, Jack the Ripper was shown on television eight times in one week, at times particularly available to children and young people. On Saturday it was shown at noon, immediately after a program specifically addressed to children. On Sunday it was shown twice in the time between 11:30 A.M. and 3:30 P.M. The different showings were followed by a promotion spot showing the killing of four police officers."[13]

This form of entertainment presented to children helps to desensitize them to violence. Those who suggest that this kind of presentation has no influence or impact on youth, should consider television advertising. If advertising on television increases sales then the media must have an impact on the thinking of the consumer. Would not the same hold true for general broadcasting? Would it not also send a message and have an influence? This would be especially true in the case of youngsters.

Numerous studies support the fact that the influence of the media results in a value system that idealizes violence as good, as an acceptable solution for problems, and as a means of winning.

Shortly after twenty-eight-year-old David Radnis saw the movie *The Deer Hunter* on television, he killed himself playing Russian roulette. At least twenty-eight other people shot themselves in a similar way after viewing the movie.[14]

According to Don E. Eberly,

"The content that comes from the television tutor is not encouraging. Children are being raised in a social environment drenched in violence. A 1990 study by the American Psychological Association concluded that by his or her tenth birthday, an American child typically witnesses 8,000 simulated murders and more than 100,000 other acts of simulated violence."[15]

Some social scientists believe that television exerts more power, and is probably a faster and more efficient teacher, than parents, thus reducing the effect that parents have in their efforts to teach or model appropriate character traits. The influence of television is summarized by Wertham:

"Children have absorbed and are absorbing from the mass media the idealization of violence. Not the association of violence with hate and hostility, but the association of violence with that which is good and just—that is the most harmful ingredient. We present to children a model figure to emulate and model method to follow. The model figure is the victorious man of violence. The model method is the employment of violent means. The hero's reasoning is usually only a gimmick; his violent action is very real. The child who sits down to view one of his ubiquitous Westerns or similar stories can be sure of two things: there will be foul play somewhere, and it will be solved by violence. The ideal is not the pursuit of happiness, but the happiness of pursuit... Children do not learn from these shows that 'good guys win over bad guys'; rather, they learn that violence is exciting—and, since we allow so much of it to be shown to them, that it is probably a pretty good thing.

"You cannot teach morals in a context of violence. The nonviolent moral is lost in the violent detail." [16]

In addition to violence and the values associated with violence, contemporary youth are able to entertain themselves at home and in arcades with graphically violent games. The way to win these games is to maim, disfigure and kill. Innovations in video game entertainment has replaced characters with footage of real actors, who, through the marvel of electronics or CD ROM, can be dismembered with all of the gore of real life. It seems incomprehensible that anyone would say that a seven, ten or fifteen year old is not desensitized to violence after watching, hour after hour, this graphic mayhem.

On the positive side, there is a growing interest in the area of "prosocial" television programming. Brown and Singhal writing in *The Content of America's Character,* state that "The character of our nation is not only reflected in our media culture, but is also influenced by it. Decades of research...have documented the socialization effect of the American media on popular culture." [17]

They go on to point out that educational television is expanding. In addition, they mention that there is a new movement toward prosocial television programming. Unfortunately, they say that "...much less is known about the effects of television programs that are intended to have positive social impacts..." [18]

Nonetheless, the idea that prosocial programming can influence society supports the notion that programs that entertain through violence and other anti social actions, can also shape the thinking and behavior of children.

It has been reported that in one episode of Happy Days, the Fonz fell in love with the local librarian. In order to get close to her he took out a library card. While this has not been verified, the story goes that the next day more children applied for library cards than at anytime in the history of American libraries.

Whether or not the story is totally factual is not really the point. What is important to note is that the media does influence behavior. Many children model the behavior of their "heroes" on TV and in the movies. Unfortunately, most of these heroes send the wrong message.

HOME VS. SCHOOL: WHO SHOULD TAKE THE LEADERSHIP POSITION?

Because of changes in the family, high geographic mobility, the influence of the media, and the instability of the child's environment, we can no longer successfully argue that the home—or, as others say, the home and church—is the only place where character education should take place.

Nevertheless, many people remain convinced that the home, not the school, is the institution which should assume responsibility for the teaching of values. For example, when Sandra Pohorlak asked state superintendents what they were doing about teaching values, one state superintendent replied that the home alone has the responsibility of teaching moral and spiritual values.[19] The unfortunate result of this line of reasoning is that when parents fail—as they too often do—society must pay the bill.

Several years ago, Congressman Charles E. Bennett told a Congressional Committee on Education that "the home and the church can no longer be solely relied upon. Today they are least available when most needed. These institutions today are no longer equipped to handle the job without help from our schools. Those children who are most in need of instruction are getting it least."[20]

Richard Gorsuch, professor of psychology at George Peabody College for Teachers, conducted extensive research regarding student values and their origins. He told an American Education Research Association conference that teachers were found to play a major role in value development for elementary school children.[21] He also cited previous research by Bronfenbrenner that suggested that "...the adult who spends the greatest amount of time in significant interaction with the child is likely to have the most influence."[22] His examination of our culture suggests that teachers may spend more time in "significant interaction" with children than do their parents.

The fact is, until sometime shortly before 1900, character building was believed to be an essential part of the formal educational process at all levels.

Without doubt, since education in America became public toward the middle of the nineteenth century, ethical instruction has been handicapped by accurate and inaccurate interpretations of the First Amendment provisions regarding religion. Nevertheless, in the early days of public education, the majority of educators continued to believe that moral instruction was an important part of their task.

Horace Mann (1796–1859) was one of the prime movers in creating the American system of free public education. He believed that education should be universal, nonsectarian, and free, and that its aims should be social efficiency, civic virtue, and character, rather than mere learning for the advancement of sectarian ends. [23] In 1916, John Dewey wrote, "It is a commonplace of educational theory that the establishment of character is a comprehensive aim of school instruction and disciplines." [24] Students of educational history, however, report that Dewey fell under the spell of relativistic behavioral science, and that his enthusiasm for character education waned in his later years.

Over a hundred years ago (1863), John Swett, a famous superintendent of public instruction for California, said, "That moral training is an important part of public school education, no one will deny.... And that it receives all the attention its importance demands, few will affirm."[25]

TEACHERS HAVE ENDORSED CHARACTER EDUCATION

In 1918 the Commission on Secondary Education, appointed by the National Education Association, issued what is perhaps the most historic statement ever made on the goals of public education. The statement has since been called the "Seven Cardinal Principles of Education." The principles were: health, command of fundamental processes, worthy home membership, vocation, citizenship, worthy use of leisure, and ethical character.[26]

In 1954, the National Education Association Representative Assembly adopted the following resolution:

> The National Education Association recognizes the necessity for a clear understanding of fundamental moral and spiritual values. The Association believes, that along with the home, the church, and the community, the school has a major responsibility for building this understanding into human behavior.
>
> The Association recommends that teacher education institutions and in-service programs stress consistently the methods through which these values may be developed, and urges continuing research to increase effectiveness of instruction in moral and spiritual values.[27]

Another NEA statement, issued by the organization's Research Division in November 1963, stated:

> After the establishment of the principle of separation of church and state, the tenets of specific religious groups could not be represented in public schools. Nevertheless, it has always been believed that even without a sectarian emphasis, the public schools can and should teach the moral and social ideals of conduct which contribute to harmonious human relations.[28]

In 1965, wondering if the previously mentioned 1918 goals were outmoded, the NEA conducted a teacher survey. The teachers surveyed returned an overwhelming verdict in favor of the seven cardinal principles: 85 percent of them said these principles were still a satisfactory list of major objectives in education. The teachers did not believe, however, that all principles were being given sufficient emphasis. The three greatest deficiencies mentioned were the worthy use of leisure, worthy home membership, and ethical character. [29]

Thus, educators have repeatedly recognized ethics as an important area for instruction. Unfortunately, as we have previously discussed, a wide gap exists between recognition of the need and effective implementation in most schools.

Many factors influence the character development of youth. No one segment of society is totally responsible nor is any single part of the culture totally to blame for what is perceived as a morally rudderless society.

Taking the various influencing segments of society into consideration, we must ask if any one of these has a better chance than others in increasing ethical teaching and behavior.

The simple fact is that today's society has only one common denominator. Today, the one common thread holding society together is the teacher. All children go to school!

Since this is the case, it seems that schools must reevaluate or rededicate themselves to systematic character education. Graduates who have had the benefits of character education stand a better chance of being better parents, workers and citizens. This alone can help break the cycle of violence, apathy, abuse and lack of a work ethic.

Recap:

1. The family has changed and its influence on character development has waned.
2. Change in child rearing practices also influenced how children displayed their character.

3. Changes in the philosophy of child rearing practices have resulted in anti-character education directions.
4. One of the most powerful influences on character development has been the various forms of media presentations to youth.
5. The school has emerged as the institution (common denominator) with the potential to take the lead in character development.

WHOSE VALUES SHOULD BE TAUGHT?

We sow a thought and reap an act;
We sow an act and reap a habit;
We sow a habit and reap a character;
We sow a character and reap a destiny.
William Makepeace Thackeray

When educators, parents and community members begin to discuss character, someone will generally ask "Whose values do you propose to teach?" Those who ask this question are generally concerned about the school imposing values that undercut their family or religious values. Unfortunately, they may not realize it, but they have been influenced by ethical relativism—the idea that there are no common core ethical values.

When the subject to be taught is chemistry, physics, or astronomy, no one asks whose chemistry? Whose physics? Whose astronomy? It is assumed that the teacher will simply present the available information to the best of his or her ability. Everyone assumes that there is an objective reality about these subjects, in spite of the fact that our understanding of the physical sciences is neither complete nor exact.

As mentioned in Chapter 3 the question, "whose values," implies that there is no objective reality about values and this is exactly what the ethical relativists claim.

The influence of this relativistic, value-free point of view is il-
lustrated by this statement of Dr. Lewis Mayhew in an address given
when he became president of the Association of Higher Education:
"Colleges are not churches, clinics nor even parents. Whether or not
a student burns a draft card, participates in a civil rights march,
engages in premarital sexual activity, becomes pregnant, attends
church, sleeps all day or drinks all night, is not really the concern
of an educational institution."[1]

The problem with this point of view is that it is not realistic
and leads to increasing crime and violence and other costly manifestations of social disintegration. Not to mention that it is a totally
irresponsible point-of-view. There *are* basic ethical principles that
are necessary to social progress, and these principles must be identified, discussed and taught.

The question of *whose values* are to be included in educational
programs is, in fact, the wrong question. In relation to schools, especially public schools, the appropriate question should be *what
values* are to be included in character education programs?

To answer the "What" question it is necessary to think of character education as having four strands. In this country strand one
consists of those principles embodied in the Constitution, Bill of
Rights and other founding documents. These principles include such
matters as justice, rights and responsibilities of citizenship, the Free-
doms (press, assembly, religion, etc.) and other principles upon
which this nation operates. Character education requires that teachers not only teach about these principles, but they must also
advocate them. For example, freedom of speech is better than cen-
sorship and justice is better than injustice.

Strand two relates to common core or consensus values. It is
possible, and has been demonstrated many times, that very diverse
groups of individuals can come to agreement as to a common set
of values that promote civility. These values consist of honesty, respect for self and others, perseverance, courage, etc. As with the first
strand these core values are to be taught and advocated. We must

inform children and adults that honesty is a standard and that it is better than dishonesty. We need to remember that *children cannot heed a message they have not heard.*

The third strand relates to group, community or cultural values. These can include issues such as the number of liquor stores in a community or the distribution of condoms at a high school. Educators are free to teach about, or discuss these values. However, in the public sector (public schools) they are not to be advocated. We can teach about the issue of gun control, but not promote the position of one group or another.

Finally, the fourth strand relates to personal values. Public sector educators can teach comparative political parties or comparative religion; however, they cannot promote one over the other. They cannot use the classroom to indoctrinate.

In California, the Los Angeles city school system has developed a teacher's guide for ethical instruction that includes this introductory statement:

> *People of every culture in every age have expressed their ideals in innumerable ways. The Los Angeles Unified School District here seeks to translate into understanding and action certain concepts that are based on the heritage of the past, and describe values of our ever-evolving society: integrity, courage, responsibility, justice, reverence, love, and respect for law and order are among these concepts.*[2]

THE ASPEN DECLARATION

In July of 1992, a significant meeting occurred in Aspen, Colorado. Educators, youth leaders, ethics scholars and other professionals came together for three and one half days to determine whether or not they could agree upon a common language that would enable personnel working with youth to use the same basic common core values. The gathering has become known as the Aspen Conference.

It resulted in the unanimously endorsed statement called **The Aspen Declaration.**

According to Michael Josephson of the Joseph & Edna Josephson Institute of Ethics,

> "The power of this statement is its articulation of a compelling need for all adults and social institutions to become more consciously involved in the development of the character of the next generation and, even more profoundly, in its establishment of a common language to describe character and ethics. The Declaration lists six core ethical values which form the foundation of democratic society..."[3]

These six core values, which are trustworthiness, respect, responsibility, fairness, caring and citizenship go directly to answering the question of "What values should be taught?"

Josephson is careful to point out that these six Pillars of Character, as they are referred to, are in no way a definitive list. Rather, they are the starting point, a common ground to begin the discussion of character education in the schools and the community.

The Aspen Declaration.

The declaration states 8 principles which are:
1. The next generation will be the stewards of our communities, nation, and planet in extraordinarily critical times.
2. The present and future well-being of our society requires an involved, caring citizenry with good moral character.
3. People do not automatically develop good moral character; therefore, conscientious efforts must be made to help young people develop the values and abilities necessary for moral decision-making and conduct.
4. Effective character education is based on core ethical values which form the foundation of democratic society; in

particular, respect, responsibility, trustworthiness, caring, justice and fairness and civic virtue and citizenship.

5. These core ethical values transcend cultural, religious, and socio-economic differences.

6. Character education is, first and foremost, an obligation of families; it is also an important obligation of faith communities, schools, youth and other human service organizations.

7. These obligations to develop character are best fulfilled when these groups work in concert.

8. The character and conduct of our youth reflect the character and conduct of society; therefore, every adult has the responsibility to teach and model the core ethical values and every social institution has the responsibility to promote the development of good character.[4]

The Aspen Conference spawned the creation, by the Joseph & Edna Josephson Institute of Ethics, "THE CHARACTER COUNTS! Coalition." The Coalition articulates the six core ethical values of the Aspen Declaration in the following manner:

A PERSON OF CHARACTER... IS TRUSTWORTHY. TREATS PEOPLE WITH RESPECT. IS RESPONSIBLE, IS FAIR, IS CARING, IS A GOOD CITIZEN

Honesty
DO: tell the truth; be sincere.
DON'T: betray a trust, deceive, mislead, cheat, or steal; don't be devious or tricky.

Integrity
DO: stand up for your beliefs; be your best self; walk your talk; show commitment, courage, and self-discipline.
DON'T: do anything you think is wrong,

Promise-Keeping

DO: keep your word and honor your commitments; pay your debts and return what you borrow.

Loyalty

DO: stand by, support and protect your family, friends, and country.

DON'T: talk behind people's backs; spread rumors or engage in harmful gossip; don't do anything wrong to keep or win a friendship or gain approval; don't ask a friend to do something wrong.

RESPECT FOR OTHERS

DO: judge all people on their merits; be courteous and polite, tolerant, appreciative and accepting of individual differences; respect the right of individuals to make decisions about their own lives.

DON'T: abuse, demand, or mistreat anyone; don't use, manipulate, exploit or take advantage of others.

RESPONSIBILITY

Accountability

DO: think before you act; consider the consequences on all people affected; think for the long term; be reliable; be accountable; accept responsibility for the consequences of your choices; set a good example for those who look up to you.

DON'T: make excuses, blame others for your mistakes or take credit for others achievements.

Excellence

DO: your best and keep trying; be diligent and industrious.
DON'T: quit or give up easily.

Self-Restraint

DO: exercise self-restraint and be disciplined.

FAIRNESS

DO: treat all people fairly; be open-minded; listen to others; try to understand what they are saying and feeling; make decisions which affect others only after appropriate considerations.

DON'T: take advantage of others' mistakes or take more than your fair share.

CARING

DO: show you care about others through kindness, caring, sharing and compassion, live by the Golden Rule and help others.

DON'T: be selfish, mean, cruel or insensitive to others feelings.

CITIZENSHIP

DO: play by the rules; obey laws; do your share; respect authority; stay informed; vote; protect your neighbors; pay your taxes; be charitable; help your community by volunteering service; protect the environment; conserve natural resources.[5]

Educators, parents and community members must go beyond the counter-productive arguments of whose values schools are going to impose upon my child. This issue is not related to personal or religious preferences. Nor is it the agenda of some secret organization or cult. It is much broader and reflects the reality that all civilized people must accept a core of commonly held beliefs and convictions. A family, a nation or a society in civilization cannot endure if there is not a thread of common values holding it together. Children are not born knowing this common core of values and expectations. These agreed upon concepts, ideas, expectations, behavior (values) must be taught in the home, the community and the classroom.

Recap

1. Asking "whose" values will schools teach is the wrong question.

2. The important question is "What" values will be taught.

3. There are common core values that all communities, nations, races, creeds, etc. can agree upon.

IS CHARACTER EDUCATION FEASIBLE?

"Education makes a greater difference between man and man than nature has made between man and brute. The virtues and powers to which men may be trained, by early education and constant discipline, are truly sublime and astonishing."

John Adams

Many people are skeptical about the feasibility of direct, systematic character education. Some say that it cannot be done, others believe that character is "caught but not taught," and a third point of view is that it cannot be taught without reference to religion. In addition, there are many who believe that this instruction should be left up to the parents. They believe that the school should teach the basics and the family should teach values.

As an example of this thinking, Dr. Max Rafferty, when he was State Superintendent of Public Education in California, said, "Never until this time, to my knowledge, has any formal attempt been made to try to set up a code of ethics or morality; which, by necessity, has to be pretty largely separated from any sectarian religious bodies. I am not sure it can be done."[1]

On the other hand, Dr. Herbert Mayer, former President of American Viewpoint, who spent more than fifty years studying juvenile delinquency, said, "It has often been said that values cannot be taught directly. This assumption has been the cause of much failure... The unrestrained freedom and irresponsibility so prevalent in the present generation of children and young people is ample evidence for the result of this kind of education."[2]

He cited the investigations of delinquents conducted by Drs. Sheldon and Eleanor Glueck of Harvard University. "Their research reveals rather conclusively," he said, "that there is little correlation between delinquency and family income or general environmental influences. They discovered the majority of young people growing up in poor neighborhoods did not become delinquents; whereas, children coming from what appeared to be excellent environments, sometimes did become delinquents:.

"Prevention of delinquent careers," wrote the Gluecks, "as our findings suggest, is dependent upon something more specific than the manipulation of general cultural environment. It entails the structuring of integrated personality and wholesome character during the first formative years of life."[3]

Scholars opposed to systematic ethical instruction often cite the historic work of Professors Hugh Hartshorne and Mark May (1928-30). Their studies failed to produce any positive evidence that character education classes conducted by schools, churches, or the Boy Scouts caused better behavior.[4]

In 1940, Professors Robert Peck and Robert Havighurst, dissatisfied with the method used by Hartshorne and May, undertook a new study. Their extensive studies of school children, over a period of sixteen years led to more optimistic conclusions. Character, they found, was definitely learned.

"Since character structure," they state, *"and even specific, detailed ways of acting, appear largely learned by emulation of the attitudes and behavior of those few people who are emotionally essential to the growing child, it seems evident that moral preaching which is not backed by consonant behavior is largely a waste of time and effort. Indeed, it may often be worse than useless if it teaches children to say one thing and do another...*

Children do as we do, not as we say. Their character tends to be an accurate reflection of the way their parents act toward them."[5]

In 1990 the Jefferson Center For Character Education and the Los Angeles Unified School District commenced a one year study to determine the effectiveness of systematic character education in the Unified School District. A broad cross section of 25 schools from across the district were chosen. The schools represented 3 elementary and 1 junior high from each of the district clusters. All the schools had diverse populations and represented a broad economic spectrum.

Prior to the end of the 1989-90 school year and the beginning of the 1990-91 school year, teaching staff in all participating schools were trained in the use of a systematic character education curriculum and the program was implemented at the beginning of the academic year.

A private consulting firm conducted evaluations of staff and student attitudes and collected data regarding various aspects of student behavior. These indicators included: frequency of major and minor disciplinary referrals, suspensions, tardies and unexcused absences. The evaluation process was designed to compare the pervious school year (1989-90) with the test year. The character education curriculum and training was the only major change in the 25 schools.

The executive summary presented by the independent evaluation firm, California Survey Research, states: [6]

DISCIPLINE PROBLEMS IN THE SCHOOLS

All forms of reported discipline problems decreased in each of the 25 schools, from the academic year before the start of the program (the Fall 1990 semester) to the end of the first year of the program (the Spring 1991 semester). The biggest drop in discipline problems was in the number of tardy students sent to the office each month. The next

biggest decrease was in the number of minor problems, followed by the number of students sent to the office for major
disciplinary problems, involving such things as fighting,
drugs, or weapons. The figures reported below are from
school records and based on actual occurrences. Because of
the large variance of occurrences, only the median response
for each question is reported. The median is a computed
numeric value such that one-half of the administrators surveyed reported figures that are below the median, and
one-half of the administrators surveyed reported figures that
are above the median.

THE RESULTS

Median Of The Reported Number Of ...	FALL 1990	SPRING 1991	% CHANGE
Major disciplinary problems in an average month.	20.0	15.0	-25.0 %
Minor disciplinary problems in an average month.	42.5	26.0	-38.8 %
Suspensions in past academic year.	50.0	42.0	-16.0 %
Tardy students sent to office per month.	50.0	30.0	-18.2 %
Students with unexcused absences sent to office per month	27.5	22.5	-18.2 %

See Appendix A for a more complete statement of the conclusions of this research.

In a second study conducted by the Learning Research and Development Center at the University of Pittsburgh the STAR
Character Education Project was independently evaluated. The
STAR Character Educator program is a school-wide character education process.

The staff report from the Learning Research and Development
Center reports:

THE PITTSBURGH STUDY

This research project addressed character education from the point of view that an important element for students is to give them a process for making ethical decisions. STAR is an acronym which stands for Stop, Think, Act and Review and constitutes the problem solving/decision making element of an overall character education program.

EXECUTIVE SUMMARY

The Values of Character: Summary examines the nature and effectiveness of the **STAR** character education program that has been widely adopted by school districts across the country. The **STAR** program of the *Jefferson Center for Character Education* is aimed at teaching the first-R, Responsibility, and thereby creating a more positive, disciplined school environment.

Two Pittsburgh foundations, the Scaife Family Foundation and the Vera I. Heinz Foundation, funded an independent evaluation of the effectiveness of the **STAR** program in use in a number of Pittsburgh area schools. Professors Judith McQuaide, Joyce Fienberg and Gaea Leinhardt, with the University of Pittsburgh School of Education, conducted the study. Data were collected during one academic year in three elementary schools which serve very different populations (suburban, urban, and inner-city), and which are considered to be exemplars of **STAR** program use. The analysis focused on **STAR** lessons delivered to 5th graders on the grounds that students in their last year of elementary school would have been exposed to the **STAR** program the longest and would represent the most complete picture of what the program can do.

In their report, released in October 1994, the LRDC researchers state "**Although teaching the concepts of good** character to public school students is not new, the increase in attention focused on character education is a relatively recent phenomenon as school districts throughout the country add character education programs to the curriculum. This increase indicates that a growing number of educators perceive a need for such programs." "Attempts to determine the effectiveness of such programs," the report states, "are few and far between... with most program evaluations in this area coming primarily from the program developers themselves."

The LRDC professors chose to evaluate the **STAR** program because of its widespread acceptance and use in their local area as well as elsewhere throughout the country. In order to understand and evaluate whether the program worked, the researchers conducted extensive observations of the program in action as well as in-depth interviews with students, teachers and school principals.

Data were collected from three very different schools which are not named to protect their right to confidentiality.

SAMPLE SCHOOLS

School	Students Staff	School 4th Grade	Percent Enrollment	Percent Non-White	Low Income
Students Suburban	22.4	57	383	1.31	37.2
Urban	10.5	30	187	52.94	36.9
Inner-City	37.0	82	576	65.97	63.6

Answers were sought to the following questions:
1. What are the perceived needs for this program in each school?
2. What are the critical components of successful program use?
3. Does the program meet the local needs?
4. What are students' understandings of the program?

RESEARCH CONCLUSIONS

The research team reached the following conclusions.

- The **STAR** program is logical in concept, is comprehensive, easy to use, and does not need to interfere with other curriculum demands.
- Because the **STAR** program addresses what most would consider to be universal values, the program can meet the needs of diverse school situations and populations, Regardless of the size of the school or the nature of its student population, no one argues against the need for students to have a sense of respect, responsibility, concern for others, and for reinforcement of ethical behaviors. All of the school personnel we interviewed felt that the **STAR** program met their local needs.
- One concern is finding ways to promote the program so that other principals will want to adopt and use it. Each principal knew of schools in which the program was not effective because of lack of commitment.
- Overall, the findings indicated that the **STAR** program was a highly valued, language-based, social skills program which had a strong, positive influence on behavior of students in each school. In addition to the specific skills and themes of the **STAR** program, its ease of use and adaptability were significant to its success.

See Appendix B for additional results.

Since 1982, Eric Schaps and researchers at the Child Development Project (CDP) in San Ramon, a suburban Northern California community, have been developing and testing a project to build student character.

The project is designed to help teachers and parents nurture characteristics such as helpfulness, fairness and responsibility.

There are five elements to the program. When combined in a consistent way in school and at home, they provide children with a clear set of expectations and supportive atmosphere for achieving them.

The five elements are: cooperative activities, helping and sharing activities, setting positive examples, understanding others and positive discipline.

Ongoing research clearly indicates that the students involved in the CDP character education program surpass comparison students in supportive and friendly behavior, proportion of positive behavior to all behavior, spontaneous helping, caring and cooperation and general harmoniousness.

In 1985, the San Ramon School District released the California Assessment Program scores for all schools in the district. The results showed the program students scored better than comparison schools, in all three CAP categories—reading, written language and math.

The Child Development Project continues to expand into others communities and conducts ongoing evaluation of the students in San Ramon. Results continue to show that there are pro-social gains in the program schools and an increase or maintenance in academic skills.

There are many examples of the feasibility of teaching values and character. Mt. Lebanon, Pa., San Ramon, Ca, the Personal Responsibility Education Program (PREP) in St. Louis, Mo. and the Los Angeles Unified School District are a few examples of effective character education programs. While these projects demonstrate that positive change does occur when systematic character education is introduced into the school, the jury is still out. There is simply a lack of hard research evidence to support the positive experience of on-site education. One of the most important elements in the continuation of the character education movement is the critical need for systematic research in this area.

When the question is asked "Is systematic character education in public schools effective?" The answer for elementary schools is an unequivocal **yes**.

However, at this point not enough research has been conducted at the Jr. High and High School levels to determine the extent to which character education programs might be effective. Nonetheless, considering the seriousness of the present day situation, it is the authors' belief that it is *never* too late to address systematic character education as one tool for educators to use in maintaining discipline and fostering responsibility in the classroom. In fact, to do *nothing* would be inexcusable and unprofessional and would certainly not be in the best interests of our young people.

Recap:

1. Early research shows that students can learn value and character traits through the teaching-learning process.
2. There is emerging evidence that character education can be taught.
3. Character education has proven to be most successful at the K-6 level and there needs to be more teaching and research at the middle and high school levels.

HOW TO TEACH CHARACTER

In proportion, as the structure of a government gives force to public opinion, it is essential that public opinion is enlightened.

George Washington

How should schools approach the task of teaching character and ethical values? Perhaps the logical starting point is for teachers and administrators to become familiar with the information contained in this book and others of its kind. They need to be familiar with the laws in their state and county pertaining to values education. They should know the history of character instruction and the benefits that may be derived from such instruction. They need to discover what other educators are doing and what programs are available.

The California School Boards Association (CSBA) created a character education task force, and in August 1982, this group issued a report titled "*A Reawakening: Character Education and the Role of the School Board Member.*" "Ethics," the report states, "can and should be taught. Schools share this responsibility with all society... Although parents are the *first* role models for children, teachers are the second. Teachers must reinforce signals that enable children to distinguish between right and wrong. Our society (and every society throughout the centuries) has established codes of ethics common to all."[1]

The task force urged California school boards to take the following steps to promote character education in the schools:

- Boards should assume responsibility for character education. Historically, public education for all in America has been justified by the need in a democratic society for literate, informed, and moral citizens.
- The electorate is accusing the schools of neglecting to teach character education. Therefore, based on historical precedent and the demands of the community that the schools serve, we should assume the leadership in reaffirming the role of the schools in character education.
- Boards should conduct a needs assessment in the community. We recognize that each community is unique. Therefore, each district should involve its community in determining the need for character education and the direction the program should take. Boards should be willing to set acceptable standards for behavior in the schools. We affirm the following statement made in the Violence and Vandalism Report published by CSBA in 1982 regarding lack of discipline:

> "If we have learned anything over the years, it is that it is almost impossible to impose standards. All groups that are going to be affected by the standards must buy into them. Discipline and control policies should be developed and implemented by school personnel, parents, and students working together. Communications should not be left to chance. Discipline policy must give firm and positive direction. Local school rules and regulations must identify standards of behavior that are clear, concise, and easily understood by parents, teachers, and students. The ultimate goal should be to train students to have self-direction and self-control."[2]

- Boards of education should develop policies and guidelines to enable students to achieve the goals of character education.[3]

Herbert C. Mayer, when president of American Viewpoint, said that a starting point for character education, was to recognize that values were not caught and therefore must be taught. His organization developed and tested a successful character education course in Ossining, New York. One conclusion was that its approach should not be dogmatic or punitive. Although even this, Dr. Mayer said, "...might be preferable to the moral vacuum which frequently exists... Whatever the disadvantages of child training of past generations with regimentation and harsh discipline, those youngsters knew what was expected of them. They may not have understood why they were expected to do some things, but they knew that they had to do them or suffer the consequences. They had a code of behavior even though it may have been imposed on them. Today few of our youngsters have anything faintly resembling a code of morals. Literally, they do not know what is right or wrong."[4]

Dr. Mayer went on to say that the actual teaching of values is not difficult. He listed four essential steps: "Identification of a value, examination of it, choice or rejection of it as related to one's point of view, and actual practice of it in everyday life."[5]

His American Viewpoint staff, working in cooperation with classroom teachers in the Ossining school system, developed a set of basic character education guidelines:

- That there was evident and imperative need for teaching moral and ethical values to growing children.
- That the classroom is one of the best situations in which such teaching can be done.
- That the teaching should be in the context of the Social Studies, not as an additional subject.

- That suitable materials must be found to supplement the regular curriculum.
- That the traditional method of "moralizing" is to be avoided.
- That specific values should be taught at the appropriate time in the development of children.
- That the program should combine real experience, vicarious experience, reading, studying, discussion, and practice.
- That teachers be encouraged to experiment and be alert to desirable teaching situations.
- That there must be direct teaching of values in order to have them take root and change behavior.[6]

The Ossining character guidelines have held up over time.

However, the current discussion of the methods for teaching character does include an argument as to whether or not character education shall be totally infused within other curriculum, i.e. social studies, or presented to students as a stand alone additional subject.

One answer to this debate is that the subject should be initially taught as a stand alone subject, in all grades, and then infused into all of the general curriculum.

It is argued that students must first master the language and concepts and then relate this knowledge to the other subjects to which they are exposed. It is difficult for some students and even some teachers to discuss subtle values issues when they are not aware of the underlying concepts and principles within the content.

Within the educational reform movement there are strong suggestions that good character must be taught "on purpose."

In *Caught In The Middle , Educational Reform for Young Adolescents in California Public Schools,* the following recommendation is presented:

1. Teachers, counselors, curriculum leaders, and those who provide their professional training should elevate issues related to the moral and ethical struggles of young adolescents

to a much higher level of concern. Attention should be given to the ideals of hard work, personal responsibility, honesty, cooperation, self-discipline, freedom, appreciation of human diversity, and the importance of education. Questions related to reality, truth, goodness, and beauty should be brought to the foreground of studies in the core, elective and exploratory curricular, including, but not limited to, literature, history, civics, science, and visual and performing arts. Ways of achieving this goal include:

    a. Revisions in curriculum guides and instructional materials which focus attention on the significance of reasoned moral and ethical choices.

    b. Provision for assignments which involve students in thinking about the moral and ethical struggles of literary and historical personalities and the potential meaning of those experiences in shaping their own ideals.

    c. Provision of in-service training opportunities for teachers, counselors and administrators which address ways of responding to the moral and ethical struggles of young adolescents through the content of various core curriculum subjects.

2. Principals, teachers and counselors should demonstrate by example, advice and instruction the ways in which personal decisions are influenced through moral reasoning based on personal and professional ideals.

3. Principals, teachers, counselors and parents should encourage and guide students to develop a vision of what they hope to be like as adults and to consider how this vision related to moral and ethical choices which are made during early adolescence. The literary and historical figures and themes found in the varied subjects of the core curriculum, as well the individual experiences and observations of students themselves, should be employed in addressing this goal."[7]

CHARACTER EDUCATION: PRINCIPLES, PROCESS AND PRACTICE

Character education, as we currently refer to the teaching and practice of values, was historically the function of the family with support from schools. Generally, children were told what was right and what was wrong and when they questioned the parent or teacher they were told, more often than not, "Because I said so!" or "Just do as you are told, or, "Children are to be seen and not heard." Children learned to be honest. When dishonest they generally "got it" both at school and at home.

As we moved through the 50s and into the 60s the shift to "questioning authority" by children began. Young parents, university professors, psychologists and teachers began to explain to children the reasons for being respectful, honest or kind. If they could not explain it to the satisfaction of the child, they felt guilty and the child did "his own thing." With this, the Dr. Spock era, as some refer to it, came the idea that children could decide what action to take by themselves without regard for personal or social consequences. Parents were taught that children had to learn to "make choices" and schools embraced the values clarification movement, which not only taught students to make choices but also suggested that all choices were OK. It was the *process* that was important, not the choice.

Of course, many factors influenced these changing times. None-the-less, the more permissive attitudes of parents, schools and society did have a major influence upon this new way of thinking, behaving and valuing.

Simultaneously, the education departments in many universities began to suggest that education was value-free. Teacher education students were taught that teachers should teach students how to make a decision but refrain from making a judgment about the "good" or "bad" choice. As a result a gradual shift in the teaching of character moved from teaching right from wrong without discussion or explanation to teaching that right and wrong were not as important as knowing how to make your decision. Everything became relative to the situation (situational ethics) and social and personal responsibility declined.

Leaders in the fledging character education movement saw the fallacy and dangers in values clarification and began to stress a return to systematic teaching of core values.

However, for many reasons, society was not prepared to abandon the process of youthful decision-making, and return to the *"Do it because I said so"* era.

While it would have been inappropriate, if not impossible to return to a previous time, there was, in the minds of many, a need to strike a balance. It seemed to many, the authors included, that decision-making was appropriate and needed. However, there emerged a perception that there was a need for parents and educators to instill principles of right and wrong.

THE THREE P'S OF CHARACTER EDUCATION

Current thinking suggests that in considering how to teach character education it is important to take three basic elements into account. These components or elements consist of principles, process and practice:

Principle: The Six Pillars of Character of the Character Counts Coalition are excellent examples of establishing principles from which a curriculum can be created. From the basic agreed upon principles of trustworthiness, respect, responsibility, fairness, caring and citizenship a basic curriculum can be developed. As lessons are created, other subprinciples can be included within the framework of each major principle.

For example, under trustworthiness, a curriculum stressing honesty, integrity, keeping of promises and loyalty can be used to expand the basic principle.

In another approach, Thomas Lickona bases his work on only two principles. In his book, *Educating for Character* his focus is on two character traits which are respect and responsibility.[8] He stresses that within the framework of these two principles all other core values can be included.

While there are different approaches to teaching basic principles of good character, it is important to understand that principles are the cornerstones of an effective character education program and can not be ignored, or considered as concepts that children know when entering school.

The point must be made that many, if not the majority of students entering school, have no idea of the significance of these principles; much less the ability to translate these ideals into behavior.

Process: The second element or component of effective character education is process: The STAR, ethical problem solving model provides one tool to examine alternatives and the personal and social consequences of one's actions.

The STAR model is taught to students in order to give them a process or system to think through their potential actions and choose the best possible alternative. It is also a valuable tool in peer mediation, conflict resolution and as a means for reviewing past actions. The process consists of four basic steps: Stop, Think, Act, Review.

There are other examples of this type of problem solving model. For example, Young People's Press, in their Books of Responsibility, use a similar process entitled STOP. However, STAR will be used here for purposes of illustration.

The following is an example of how the STAR model can be utilized as a problem-solving skill. The instructional process is to teach students to:

Stop: Take the appropriate amount of time to think through the action about to be taken or to look at the action taken.

Think: Make a mental list of options that are available in a particular situation.
   a. What are my alternatives?
   b. What behavior will I choose?
   c. What might be the consequences.

Or make a list of actions taken.
   a. What could have been my alternatives?
   b. What did I do?
   c. What will be the consequences.

Act: Choose the best alternative and take appropriate action. I am choosing to _____. Or note what action I chose. I chose to _____.

Review: Ask, "**Will** my action get me closer to or further from my goals and how will it affect others?" or ask, "**Did** my action get me closer to or further from my goals and how did it affect others?"

Example 1: After an incident.

A boy in the yard at a STAR school is observed pushing another boy. He is approached by the playground supervisor and the following dialogue ensues.

Yard supervisor:	Let's STAR what just happened with you and Joey.
Boy:	Ok. I pushed him because he took my hat.
Yard supervisor:	Did you stop and think before you pushed him?
Boy:	No.
Yard supervisor:	Let's do that now so you will know what to do the next time this happens. What will you do next time?
Boy:	I'll stop and think.

Yard Supervisor:	What will you think about?
Boy:	Ways to handle the problem.
Yard supervisor:	What might they be?
Boy:	I could push him and take my hat back or I could come and tell you.
Yard supervisor:	What will happen in each case?
Boy:	I'll probably be in trouble again if I push him. If I tell you I'll get my hat back and won't be in trouble.
Yard supervisor:	Ok! so, let's review what just happened.
Boy:	I didn't come and tell so now I have to sit on the STOP bench for five minutes.

Example 2: Planning ahead.

There are two minutes to go before class is over.

Teacher:	Class! What does STAR mean?
Class:	Stop, think, act and review!
Teacher:	Good! Let's pretend there is a dollar lying on the floor. Use the second step in STAR and choose what you can do.
Student A:	I could pick it up and put it in my pocket.
Teacher:	Let's review that choice. What might be the consequences of your action?
Student B:	I would be happy because I had a dollar.
Student C:	Yeah! But the person who lost it would be sad or in trouble.
Teacher:	Are there any other alternatives?
Student D:	Pick it up and turn it in.
Teacher:	Let's review that choice. What might be the consequences if you turned it in?
Student E:	If no one claimed it I might get it back.
Student F:	The person who lost it would feel good.
Student G:	I would feel good because I gave it back.

Teacher:	Which do you think is the best alternative in this case.
Class:	Turn it in!
Teacher:	Ok! Good! Let's go to recess.

Practice: The third component in an effective character education program is to translate the principles into behavior practices that can be performed by the students. This is not unlike math. A teacher will teach the principles and concepts and the students will go to the chalkboard, complete worksheets and do homework as a means of perfecting these skills.

One Curriculum, Responsibility Skills, provides lessons focused on measurable behaviors that can be practiced and that foster personal and social responsibility. *Be Prepared, Be on Time, Be A Doer, Be a Goal Setter,* etc. all have character consequences that impact on the individual and society. These practices are derived from principles that were cited above.

For Example:

In translating the fundamental principle, Respect, into practice teachers will discuss the meaning of respect and how it affects the individual, classroom, school or society. The class is given the opportunity to discuss why it is important to be respectful and the benefits of respectful behavior.

The students can then use STAR to look at a situation and determine the positive and negative consequences of respectful or disrespectful behaviors.

The teacher could use the following situation as an example. Someone is disrespectful to you by calling you a dirty name. What is the process you will need to go through before you react?

A student's response might be, "I will stop and think about my (A, B, C) alternatives, the behavior I will choose and what might be the consequences. I will know that when I make my choice, when

I act upon my decision, I am choosing to behave in such a way and therefore I am responsible for my behavior. I should take the time to review my actions by asking myself, "Did (will) my actions get me closer to or further from my goals (personal responsibility) and how did (will) my behavior affect those around me (social responsibility)?"

Of course, no student would give a respond in this pure academic language. Kids just don't talk that way. The point is that student can develop a thinking process, a language, that will support ethical problem solving.

Moving from this discussion, the teacher can now take the class or individual to the next level. That is, the translation from an idea to a concrete, observable behavior. For example, the following discussion might take place.

Teacher:	What are some responsibility skills that you can practice that will show respect?
Students:	We can be On Time so the teachers can start teaching.
	We can be quiet (Be a Listener) while others are speaking.
	We can pay attention (Be Here) when the teacher is talking.

After developing their list, students can practice the behaviors and the teacher can acknowledge and reinforce the positive actions of the students. In some cases, the class might actually post this list as a reminder that they have chosen these respectful behaviors.

A second example of integrating the 3 P's of effective character education is found in another curriculum titled, *LESSONS IN CHARACTER*.[9]

Young People's Press in San Diego, California has taken the Six Pillars of Character that were decided upon at the Aspen Conference (Chapter 6) and refined by the CHARACTER COUNTS!

Coalition of the Josephson Institute of Ethics and developed a multicultural, literature based curriculum.

These *LESSONS IN CHARACTER* include the three elements of character education listed above and a broad array of multicultural children's stories. These stories are used to illustrate the principles embodied in the Six Pillars of Character: Trustworthiness, Respect, Responsibility, Fairness, Caring and Citizenship.

The *LESSONS IN CHARACTER* curriculum is divided into three elements or components. As mentioned above, the first consists of the principles which are based on the Six Pillars. The second includes thinking activities that foster the development of the language and concepts associated with these values and the third relates to practicing observable behaviors such as *Be a good neighbor, Be a person who shares, Be a polite person and Be an honest person.*

The lesson plans, for lessons in character, include a unit for each of the Six Pillars. Within each unit are four lessons which concentrate on defining and practicing the principal and skill in school, the home and the community.

For example, under the Pillar, Responsibility, there is a third grade unit on Be A Goal Setter. Within this unit are four lessons.

Lesson 1

MAIN IDEA:
Setting goals is a three step process. Following the steps helps you reach your goal.

LEARNER OBJECTIVES:
Students will:
• define the term goal
• list the steps in the goal-setting process
• discuss the benefits of being a goal-setter
• identify people who can be helpful in working toward your goals

Lesson 2

MAIN IDEA:
Being a goal setter at school can help you make important improvements in your performance and in your relationships with others.

LEARNER OBJECTIVES:
Students Will:
- identify areas in which they can set goals for themselves at school
- use goal setting as a problem-solving method
- set a goal for themselves related to school

Lesson 3

MAIN IDEA:
When you are a goal setter, you can make improvements in yourself and in you life, and you can try new ways of doing things. You know how to use your time wisely, and you know what to expect will happen. Goal setters feel confident, and know they can trust a goal setter to live up to promises.

LEARNER OBJECTIVES:
Students will:
- relate feelings to being or not being a goal setter
- discuss the personal benefits of being a goal setter

Lesson 4

MAIN IDEA:
Goal setting at home can help you to solve problems or make improvements. Goal setters in the community contribute to one's well-being.

LEARNER OBJECTIVES:

Students will:

- identify areas in which they can set goals at home and in the community
- set a specific goal for themselves related to life at home
- talk with community members about how their jobs involve goal setting that is helpful to the whole community.

Each of these MAIN IDEAS and LEARNER OBJECTIVES are followed by TEACHING STRATEGIES that include thinking and doing.

The teacher's management guide also suggests a class project that relates to the MAIN IDEA. For example, this particular Pillar, Responsibility, and the related Goal Setting lessons has the following class project:

Ask the students to come up with a goal for the entire class to work toward. Write the goal on the *Be a goal setter poster.* Then work together to fill in the checkpoints as the class accomplishes each step toward goal attainment.

A poster is provided with a place to write in the goal. For the remainder of the month, the class works on achieving this goal. Students record progress toward reaching their goal on the classroom poster. This, of course, is an example of translating the principle or concept into action or practice.

SHOULD CHARACTER EDUCATION BE A STAND-ALONE SUBJECT?

Many educators believe that character instruction should be woven into the overall curriculum rather than be treated as a separate subject. This may be a worthy ideal, and it certainly was the case many years ago in the days of the McGuffey Reader. "As recently as twenty-five years ago," stated Dr. John Silber in 1980, "citizenship education, that is, education of the child in morals and civic duty, was the central core and focus of all primary and secondary education. It was what education was about." [10]

The problem with the idea that values should be woven into the curriculum is that this would entail a huge and expensive revision of most present school textbooks. Unfortunately, value or character content has disappeared from many school texts. During the past 25-30 years many publishers have shied away from value content in favor of factual content.

In view of this, we need to ask the question: "If character education is as important as reading, writing, and arithmetic, as the authors insist, then why shouldn't it be taught specifically, systematically, and separately?"

A second problem is the misconception that character education is being taught in classrooms without the need for a specific lesson plan. When teachers are asked if they teach about honesty, for example, they generally reply in the affirmative. However, when questioned further, they often admit that the teaching of honesty occurs following a dishonest act. Additionally, when asked for their lesson plan for honesty they cannot provide one. Math, science, social studies and reading are not taught haphazardly, nor should character education be treated in that manner. Good character education should be taught deliberately.

The systematic, stand-alone teaching of character does not mean that character instruction is deleted from other academic areas. All academic studies can contribute to fostering good character. The "stand alone" teaching of the principles, process and practices of good character is a first step which can lead to infusion into the general curriculum and the culture of the school.

As a class or school moves from the specific "on purpose" teaching of the principles of good character, many other areas of the curriculum open up to the inclusion of character education.

Examples from history and the study of the lives of great men and women are methods of teaching character that were once widely used in American schools and is still used in other countries. One reason that American schools no longer use history, according to Benson and Engeman, is that "John Dewey expressly opposed it in *Democracy in Education.*"[11]

Plutarch's Lives, according to Benson,

> "...*includes comments on the virtues and vices of the subject of the biography;* The Lives of the Saints *has long been used in religious education. Military school curricula described the courageous exploits of their alumni, and the British public schools in England's nineteenth-century revival of morality brought back "old boys" (alumni) to the campus to encourage students to higher and more courageous ideals of public service. Religious orders commemorate their more pious deceased members; the stories of Lincoln's moral deeds can inspire young people who are interested in politics; and Parson Weems' biography of George Washington was historically inaccurate, but the stories it told may have helped many Americans to live better lives.* McGuffey's Readers, *widely employed in American public schools in the last century, include a number of historical examples of courage, honesty, gentleness, and other moral qualities.*"

Before World War II, every Japanese schoolchild memorized a code of ethics, and this was reinforced with formal daily character instruction in the classroom. Instruction consisted chiefly of stories and biographical sketches. Reed Irvine describes a typical text printed in Japan for use in Japanese schools in Hawaii:

> *The text began with a story that emphasized respect for parents and the importance of children avoiding actions which might bring disgrace to their families. This was followed by a chapter on Abraham Lincoln which emphasized his honesty, kindness, and sense of justice. Next came a biography of James A. Garfield, an inspiring story of his struggle to rise from the depths of poverty, a story that has probably not been read by any American*

school child (outside of Hawaii's Japanese schools for several gen-erations. This account of Garfield's life stressed the sacrifice made by his older brother to permit James to attend school, and it showed how James repaid his debt by his great diligence in both study and work. Other exemplary men of character portrayed in this text include Herbert Hoover, Admiral Togo, who won fame in the Russo-Japanese War, and the conqueror of yellow fever, Dr. Noguchi... [12]

Once the specific language or principles of good character be-come an integral part of the school culture there are many opportunities for the use of supplementary curriculum and materi-als that enhance regular classroom instruction.

One outstanding series of biographies parents and teachers can use as a tool for helping children understand basic personal values is called *Value Tales*. This program consists of twenty attractively il-lustrated books. Each book is about a historical figure and is written to emphasize one particular value or character trait: the life of Louis Pasteur teaches the value of believing in yourself; the life of Helen Keller illustrates determination; the story of the Wright brothers describes patience; and so forth.

In addition, there are numerous supplementary books for use in the school or the home. William Bennett's books related to vir-tues, values and parenting constitute important resources. Other books such as *20 Teachable Virtues* by Unell and Wycokoff (Perigee Books) and *50 Practical Ways to Take Our Kids Back from the World* by Michael J. McManus (Tyndale House Publishers) are a few of the examples of the growing library of support material.

THE SCHOOL AS AN ISLAND

In many cases, the teaching of character is confined to one class-room, a counselor, a single course or left up to the individual teacher. As a result, this lack of cohesiveness or school wide initiative dilutes the effectiveness of the systematic character curriculum.

In actuality the school can be thought of as an island. In many cases it is the most peaceful, safe and supportive island that children experience. It is helpful to think of the school as having a language and culture of its own. If the language on the island is one of dismay, despair and disdain for students or their behavior, then the general behavior of the inhabitants of the island will reflect those attitudes attendant with the language. If, on the other hand, the language promotes a culture of caring, honesty, respect, hard work achievement then the majority of the students and staff will behave in that manner.

Therefore, the optimal approach to effective teaching of character and values is to adopt a school-wide approach. This approach should include these fundamental elements.

1. The school should be viewed as an island with it's own language and culture. While it is true the school does, in fact extend into the home and the community, there remains the reality that schools are also separate from the outside world. A school can create it's own pro- character environment. In relation to character education a thematic approach can be used to focus the staff and students on a particular principle, i.e., honesty or respect.

2. The instructional component of character curriculum should be:
   a. Connected with the school-wide theme.
   b. Taught as a separate stand-alone subject **and** infused into the general curriculum.
   c. All staff should be aware of and support the school-wide theme.

3. Emphasis should be placed on how well students translate (perform) the principles into pro-social behavior.

See appendix C for a more complete discussion of the elements of a successful character education program.

The approaches to teaching character may vary from school to school and classroom to classroom. Nonetheless, it is becoming clear that character traits and values are being deliberately taught, learned and practiced in increasing numbers. The caution is that character education that is invisible, has no lesson plans, and does not include principles, process and practices is more than likely ineffective.

Someone once said that "Something that is everywhere is nowhere." Character education that is perceived to be everywhere is doomed to be less effective than character education that is specific, has objectives, an evaluation component and reinforces the good character of students and staff.

Recap

1. There are many ways to teach character. They include infusion, example, modeling and direct instruction.
2. The school reform movement in many states is including character education as one important element in the reform of public schools.
3. Effective character education has three elements. They are referred to as the Three-P's.
4. The Three-P's consist of Principles, Practices and Processes.

CHARACTER EDUCATION– WHERE ARE WE GOING FROM HERE?

If you can be well without health, you may be happy without virtue.

Edmund Burke

Systematic character education in primary and secondary schools is a remarkable bargain for the entire community. Students benefit by acquiring positive attitudes and habits that enhance their confidence and make their lives happier and more productive. Teachers' work becomes easier and more satisfying when they achieve greater classroom discipline. Parents are pleased when their children learn to be more courteous, considerate, and productive. School administrators welcome the improvements in discipline, attendance, scholarship, and student and teacher morale, as well as reductions in school vandalism.

Business people, increasingly concerned with the costs and problems they are experiencing in hiring young people who are poorly trained and disciplined, welcome programs that improve youthful attitudes and behavior in the work place.

For example, several school districts across the country are experimenting with including a CPA (Character Point Average) along with the GPA (Grade Point Average) so employers can determine the kind of person applying for a job. This character point average addresses employer concerns as to the type of person to be hired. Is the person honest, dependable, hard working; and able to make decisions? In Santa Barbara, California the high schools are currently developing and testing a student profile that addresses these employer needs. A major part of the effort will be to build business and community awareness of the profile. It will be necessary that employers ask potential employees for a copy of their CPA profile. Hopefully, as the use of such instruments come into practice students will see the need to make the connection between work habits at school and eventual employment. When character profiles are compared, according to J. R. Richards, principal, at Santa Barbara High School, the "...students with good attendance should have a better chance of getting the job when the employer compares his/her profile with students with poor attendance patterns."

Conventional wisdom suggests that there is a positive correlation between students who are self disciplined and academic performance. Given recent negative trends in scholarship, this relationship between self discipline and performance has great significance.

Numerous studies show that academic achievement in American schools has been going downhill since the early 1960s. Eggerz, in her excellent essay "Why Our Public Schools Are Failing," provides the following information:[1]

The decline in Scholastic Aptitude Test scores, which began in 1963, took its most dramatic dip in three years in 1980 when the average verbal test score was 424 compared to 427 in 1979 and 478 in 1963.

The 1963 overall test score of 502 in math sank to 466 in 1980, down from 467 in 1979.

Even more shocking than the general decline is the drop in achievement among highest scoring students. From 1979 to 1980 the number of students getting the highest SAT scores—over 750—fell from 2,650 to 1,892 in verbal areas and from 9,059 to 7,675 in math.

In fact, the number of students scoring better than 650 on college entrance exams has dropped dramatically since the early 1970s, by 46 percent. From 1972 to 1980 those scoring better than 650 on the verbal part of the SAT dropped from 53,794 to 29,019....[1] Lack of discipline in American schools leads to violence, vandalism, theft, drugs, alcohol, and reduced academic achievement, and also deprives those students who want to study in a peaceful environment the opportunity to get the most out of education. Fear and disruption in a school seriously hampers the teaching-learning process

In *Why Johnny Can't Tell Right From Wrong,* William Kilpatrick blames the decline in the ability of children to read effectively on the use of inferior teaching methodology. He sees a corresponding problem in the area of character development. He states, "A similar situation exists with regard to moral education. In addition to the fact that Johnny still can't read, we are now faced with the more serious problem that he can't tell right from wrong."

While citing figures such as "525,000 attacks, shakedowns and robberies" in schools each year. Kilpatrick writes, "These behaviors are troubling enough, but just as worrisome are the attitudes that accompany them. Many youngsters have a difficult time seeing any moral dimension to their actions: getting drunk and having sex are just things to do."[2]

If, in fact, Kilpatrick is correct then the inability to tell right from wrong not only impacts the ability of the individual to learn but also has corresponding influence of other members of the class, including the teacher. When students control their behavior, there is naturally more time to teach and learn.

According to a study by James S. Coleman, "schools with more homework, less absenteeism, and an *orderly environment* have higher achievement regardless of the family background of the students."[3]

A study by Professor Ronald Edmonds of the Harvard Graduate School of Education concluded that, "effective schools had principals who were active leaders, an *orderly climate,* an emphasis on basic skills, standardized tests to measure skills, and teachers who have high expectations for all students."[4]

In a book entitled *15,000 Hours: Secondary Schools and Their Effects on Children,* English researchers report on a thorough examination of the British secondary school system. This study concluded, "Schools do indeed have an important impact on children's development and it does matter which school a child attends."[5] The implication is that orderly schools have a greater positive influence on children as learners and future workers.

When schools in poor neighborhoods in London were compared for performance, the study showed that some schools were much better than others. Which schools were better? Those schools that maintained an *orderly environment.* Teachers in those schools expected results, and assigned and checked homework regularly.[6]

There are trends that appear to be indicative of improvement. For example the most recent SAT results (August, 1995) indicate a slight improvement in academic achievement. However, it remains to be seen whether or not the increase in academic achievement parallels the increase in systematic character education programs across the country.

RESPONSIBLE BEHAVIOR DOES PAY

Students who develop a positive code of conduct and a healthy self-image not only behave better in school, but in most cases will also become healthier, happier, more productive adults.

Many distinguished philosophers have pointed out the connection between virtuous behavior and true success—true happiness. Edmund Burke, whose quotation appears at the beginning of this chapter, is one example of this viewpoint.

Here are some similar statements by other great minds:

Were I not to follow the straight road for its straightness, I should follow it for having found by experience that in the end it is commonly the happiest and most useful track.

Michel Montaigne

If rascals knew the advantages of virtue, they would become honest men.

Benjamin Franklin

It is not the brains that matter most, but that which guides them—the character, the heart, generous qualities, progressive ideas.

Fedor Mikhailovich Dostoevski

No man is free who is not master of himself.

Epictetus

There is no truth more thoroughly established than that there exists in the course of Nature, an indissoluble union between virtue and happiness.

George Washington

THE EDUCATIONAL PENDULUM IS SWINGING

In 1975 Howard Flieger, editor of *U.S. News & World Report*,[7] said on his editorial page, "Is instruction in morals and ethics becoming more popular in the schools? There are some faint signs of it... History makes a truism of Mr. Goble's statement that a society cannot survive without a workable system of values." Unfortunately, back in 1975, this editorial seemed to arouse little interest or attention.

Several years later, however, when Marvin Stone, the new editor of *U.S. News & World Report*, wrote an editorial titled "Are Ethics on the Way Back?" the response was very different. The Jefferson Center for Character Education received more than five hundred letters of inquiry about ethical instruction. That response dramatically confirmed Mr. Stone's statement that "it has become permissible to speak, write, and think about 'ethics.' That represents a healthy advance over very recent times when anyone who talked in such terms was regarded as naive."[8]

Unfortunately, the "healthy advance" was short lived. Continuing into the 1990s the emphasis in media continued to focus on the problems that society was encountering with little discussion as to the solutions to these problems. The emphasis was clearly on the symptoms of societies' ills not the causes and certainly not the cure.

For example, a December 15, 1981 issue of *U.S. News & World Report*, carried the article "Troubled Teenagers," which cited shocking statistics on crime, suicide, illegitimacy, and alcoholism. Several "experts" were interviewed to find out what was wrong, but not one of them mentioned that our schools and colleges had virtually stopped deliberately teaching values.[9]

Nonetheless, the idea that schools, colleges and other institutions, including the family, must place greater emphasis on efforts to teach ethical values has slowly begun to regain acceptance.

The shift toward a greater discussion of the issues of teaching values or character received a dramatic boost in 1987 when the National School Boards Association published *Building Character in the Public Schools: Strategies for Success.* In the forward, Howe and Shannon quote Dean William R. Inge as saying, "The aim of education is the knowledge not of *fact* but of *values.*"[10]

A second indication of the move away from value neutral education was the fact that the 1988 booklet, *Moral and Civic Education and Teaching About Religion,* published by the California Department of Education, was republished in 1991 and distributed to all schools in California.[11]

Another step was taken when, in 1991 the American Association of School Administrators distributed a Critical Issues Report titled *Teaching Values and Ethics.*

The introduction to the report stated,

"Today, schools are asked to take on much more than the three R's. With increasing numbers of single- or two-career families, parents and other community members often don't have enough time to instill in children the values and ethics they need to be contributing members of society. Inevitably, this has led to an erosion of what most consider the traditional commitment to behaving ethically. Today's headlines confirm this: high incidence of drug and alcohol abuse, violence, gangs, acts of bigotry, embezzlement, and corruption reveal people's growing lack of respect for themselves and others."[12]

Magazines, newspaper articles and editorials on ethical instruction in the schools began to increase. The authors have a growing file of such articles. This file began to expand with a February 22, 1982 issue of the *Wall Street Journal*. The title of the article is "Teaching Morality in the Public Schools" and its author, Terry Eastland, is editor of the *Virginia-Pilot* newspaper in Norfolk. Here are typical comments from this article:

> *It has been 20 years since the Supreme Court declared in Engel vs. Vitale that state-sponsored public school prayer violates the Constitution.... Proponents of school prayer say that crime, racial conflict, drug abuse, and sexual promiscuity, among other social problems, have intensified since the Engel decision... Opponents of social prayer typically deride the idea that prayer might be thus efficacious...*
>
> *Sociologists may speculate about the cause of these problems, but fundamentally they result from a widespread absence in young people of a basic morality. This morality consists, of among other things, honesty, fairness, respect for law, courage, diligence, and respect for others. These qualities are commonly regarded as part of the Judeo-Christian ethic, but not its exclusive property....*
>
> *For more than two thousand years, Western nations have transmitted this basic morality to each new generation. The means of propagation have typically been the family, the church,*

and the schools. In the U.S., the public schools have been assigned the major share of the responsibility. But in the past two decades, the schools increasingly have failed to do this job...
   Everyone interested in the public schools should begin reviewing what is taught or failing to be taught in their schools, with a view toward making sure that the basic morality is recovered and instilled in the latest generation of students...[13]

While it is some time ago that the Wall Street Journal article was written in 1982, what is important is that it states a point of view that is not only valid in the 90s, but beginning to become mainstream thinking.

The Girl Scouts of the United States fueled the discussion in 1989 when they published the *Girl Scouts Survey on The Beliefs and Moral Values of American Children.* This extensive survey targeted over five thousand boys and girls between the fourth and twelfth grades.

The report concludes by stating,

"Finally, there needs to be a recognition that it is not enough to change the environment children inhabit. Those genuinely interested in the moral lives of children must be at least as concerned with the "whys" underlying behavior as they are with the environmental factors which shape it. Related to this, adults need to be just as concerned with the "whys" underlying behavior as they are with the "whats" of behavior. Stated differently, it is not enough to "just say no" to drugs or any other undesirable behavior. Children are capable of moral reasoning and adults would do well to cultivate this. Only then will children be equipped to deal with the difficult moral decisions they will inevitably face, the futures they worry about and the problems they will confront as citizens of a community and the nation."[14]

As problems in society worsened, the conversation regarding character began to gain momentum. Scholars began to call for action in the schools. In Teacher Magazine, Robert Coles made it very clear regarding his position of the teaching of values or character in the schools. He was quoted as stating, "At Harvard, at least until 1902, it was the mission of the college to educate men of character." He continues, "Schools are for the education of the whole person, and it is the responsibility of the schools to inculcate character." [15]

The methods of classroom teaching began to be scrutinized in relation to their role as character builders. The discussion was not purely academic. While it was generally understood that teachers taught character, the instruction in character appeared to be invisible. In spite of the fact that people thought teachers were inculcating values there was scant evidence of systematic programs or curriculum in this area of classroom instruction. As a result, the academic discussion began to find it's way into policy discourse in the schools of education. Teacher educators began to inquire where and how was character being taught? Was it included in other areas of instruction or being taught on a stand-alone subject? If character instruction was, in fact, in place how was it being evaluated?

This discourse by the academic community fueled the discussion and raised awareness.

As the discussion grew publications aimed at the practitioner began to appear. For example, the publication of *It's Elementary,* by California State Department of Education in 1992 addressed character education in the elementary school. The purpose of the document was to "...assist teachers, administrators, parents, and community leaders in achieving excellence in public schools during the most critical years of a child's educational development."[16]

The authors of the document included a section on character education. In it they state,

"Character education is not the sole responsibility of the schools. The primary influence on a child's moral formation is, and will always remain with what happens in the home. The point is, however, that parents need—and expect—all the support they can get in helping children become moral. Indeed, out of 25 possibilities listed on the Gallup Poll's annual survey of attitudes toward education in the U.S., the second highest show of approval generally is accorded to the following goals for the public schools: To develop standards of what is right and wrong. (Only the classic academic mission, to develop the ability to speak and write correctly, consistently scores higher)....beginning in the elementary years, schools have a special obligation to encourage children to adopt as their own the highest ethical standards of the community."[17]

The proliferation of articles in the late 1980s and early 90s are testament to the fact that the pendulum has indeed begun to swing toward a greater awareness of the need to reintroduce systematic character education into classrooms. The key word is systematic. Academicians, boards, administrators, teachers and researchers began to note the need to be more specific about character education curriculum. From all sectors of the educational community there was the emergence of a greater awareness that this element of effective education could no longer be left to chance.

As the conversation grew, the difficult questions were being answered. In November of 1994, The Freedom Forum First Amendment Center at Vanderbilt University published *Finding Common Ground*. This publication, edited by Charles C. Hynes, of George Mason University, is primarily "...designed to provide general information on the subject of religious expression and practices in schools." A major portion of the document is devoted to the issue of character education and additionally provides information on resources available to schools.[18] For example, it directs readers to such resources as Educational Leadership, the Journal of Association for Supervision and Curriculum Developments, which devoted an entire issue to Character Education in November, 1993.[19]

Those with questions about the issue of character education and the separation of Church and State now have a document to which they could turn for answers.

The evidence that the pendulum has moved away from value neutral education continues to accumulate. The creation of the Character Education Partnership, The CHARACTER COUNTS! Coalition, and numerous state and local organizations indicates a national movement toward character and values education. In addition articles and books continue to appear at an increasing rate.

When this book was first published in 1983 it, for the most part, stood alone. The discussion of character education in the public schools was taboo. However, today, we are encouraged by such occurrences as the House of Representatives passing House Joint Resolution 366 which calls for a week in October that will be designated a National Character Counts Week. This event occurred in 1994 and 1995 and has become established as an annual national focus on creating an awareness of character development in our schools, homes and communities. There is a growing awareness that everyone, the schools, families, community organizations and business and faith establishments are all going to have to get involved.

As a result, schools and communities across the country and in foreign lands are adopting character education programs.

One example of how this movement has spread beyond the schools is the fact that the national YMCA has established a series of character development activities for it's members. These activities are based on the Six Pillars of Character mentioned earlier in this book and demonstrate how attitudes have changed since 1983.

WHAT LAYMEN CAN DO TO HELP

Frequently, people who are not in education would like to encourage schools to do more in this regard but are not sure how to proceed.

The American system of public education is unique. In other countries, education is governed by professional educators or federal officials. The Tenth Amendment to the United States Constitution implicitly reserves the responsibility for public education to the states or to "the people." This democratic approach to education has produced a system which is usually responsive "to the people" at the local level. While it may not appear to work all of the time, it does work most of the time.

Because of the democratic nature of our public schools, changes may be initiated from a variety of sources, including boards of education; superintendents; assistant superintendents; school principals; school advisory groups and parent-teacher associations; community groups such as business-education councils, chambers of commerce, service clubs, and crime task forces; parents; teachers and other members of the staff.

Since there are many forces that mold the local schools, no single approach is best for all districts. In some districts, school boards have provided the leadership for starting character education. In other districts, it has been initiated by the superintendent or an assistant superintendent for instruction; elsewhere, principals and teachers have provided the impetus. Board members or school administrators can usually recommend the best way to present and start the program successfully.

Huffman, in *Developing a Character Education Program: One School Districts Experience*,[20] outlines step-by-step the procedures, pitfalls and remedies for the inclusion of the entire community in the development of a district-wide character education program.

Community organizations with ties to educational leaders (perhaps the superintendent or school board member belongs to the Kiwanis or Rotary or Junior League) are usually excellent starting points. Prominent business or community leaders may help to gain school interest.

It is highly desirable to involve school board and parent-teacher organizations since there may be legitimate questions from the community.

COMMUNITY BASED CHARACTER EDUCATION

One of the most significant signs of the return to the systematic teaching of character and values is the emerging trend toward the involvement of the entire community in efforts to support the teaching of values in the classroom and the school.

A number of communities across the nation have developed or are developing a community based approach to systematic character education. Towns and cities such as Milton, Vermont; Santa Ynez area of central coast of California; Tyler, Texas; Woodland Hills, Bethel Park and Mt. Lebanon in Pennsylvania are among communities that are including the schools, the business sector, law enforcement, community based organizations and the faith establishment in agreeing upon consensus core values that each sector of the community can teach and reinforce.

The CHARACTER COUNTS! Coalition has as a major goal the establishment of community-wide agreements to accept and foster, trustworthiness, respect for others, responsibility, fairness, caring and citizenship, the Six Pillars of Character. Michael Josephson, the creator of the Coalition, predicted in 1994 that over one thousand communities would embrace the Six Pillars by Character Counts Week in October, 1995. As this book is being written that goal is nearing.

One exciting example of community based character education is the effort undertaken in Duncanville, Texas.

Chief Michael Courville of the Duncanville Police Department heard of the efforts of Chief Robinson, formerly the police chief in Tyler, Texas. Chief Robinson had supported character education in the schools as a crime prevention measure. Through Chief Robinson's efforts the elementary schools initiated systematic school wide character programs in their schools and community.

In Duncanville, the Chief convinced the city council to use some of its drug seizure forfeiture money (money confiscated in drug arrests) to support a character education program in the elementary schools. His argument was clear, "character education is prevention and prevention can save tax dollars, lives and families down the road."

Using the forfeiture dollars the chief purchased curriculum and arranged for the training of teachers. In addition, he allowed several police officers, who volunteered, to attend the teacher training. Following the joint training, several of the officers volunteered to "adopt" a school and be visible around the school in the hope of catching children demonstrating good character traits. This evolved into a "caught being responsible" program where officers give certificates or "tickets" to children who they observed being responsible or who were nominated by their teachers. Drawings were conducted by the officers in the schools and the responsible students received certificates, rewards and T-shirts which were purchased by the Duncanville Police Department.

The Chief and Leslie Flanery, an administrator in the Duncanville schools, established a team that interacted with teachers, parents and the community. Through their efforts, the concept of the entire community being involved in their effort took on a life of its own. Eventually, the Chief and Mrs. Flanery were able to enlist the support of the Chamber of Commerce and other community organizations. For the 1995-96 school year, the faith community agreed to mention or preach about the monthly character education themes during their services.

The schools had agreed to adopt specific themes, such as, Be Honest, Be On Time, etc. and the various elements of the community agreed to support this school distinct effort by also promoting the theme. For example, the Chamber of Commerce printed signs for it's members that were prominently displayed in places of business as reminders to students and the community that Duncanville supports basic core values of good character.

The Duncanville Community Based Character Education Program has been expanded to include the middle schools and eventually will move into the high schools.

The importance of this effort is that this is an example of a whole "village" coming together to raise their children.

This concept of including the entire community is the school's and home efforts to instill good character in youth is not new. In fact, until 40 years ago it was more the rule than the exception. In, *The Content of America's Character,* Brooks concludes a chapter on community based character education with the following:

> *It might be asked what lessons have been learned from these early attempts at broadening character education from the school to the community.*
>
> *Character or values education has moved to a point where the majority of society is beginning to see the need for a community approach rather than an approach that leaves individual families and institutions working in isolation.*
>
> *There are difficult questions that need to be resolved. The issue of whose values versus what values is a major concern of many. How will the school interface with the community organizations such as churches, mosques, and synagogues, community based organizations, and independent youth organizations?*
>
> *How will a school or school system ensure that all segments of the community are allowed to give their input and participate informing a community-wide consensus?*
>
> *What will be evaluated and how will this be accomplished?*
>
> *Will schools create a new curriculum or use and adapt an existing program?*
>
> *Who should be involved in the planning and how should they be selected?*
>
> *In far too many cases the paramount question being asked is: Should we as a school and community be involved in character or values education at all? The answer to this question appears to rest in African wisdom. It does take an entire village to raise a child.* [21]

The effort to restore civility to society is in the beginning stages. As demonstrated in the latter part of this book we have discussed strategies that work and have given examples of a few of the many school and community efforts that can help restore such core values as trustworthiness, respect, civility, perseverance, kindness and good citizenship to mention a few.

Even though there is a rapidly growing awareness of the need to return our schools, our families and our communities to the systematic teaching of values, there is still much to be done.

The dialogue between educators and the rest of the community, including parents, must include a respectful discussion of the issues related to character education *in the schools and in the community.*

Involvement in schools and communities across the country indicate that there are many questions that **each** community or school must answer. Character education is not a package that can be handed to a school or community.

In concluding this book we have posed a few questions that can be used as a starting place for meaningful dialogue. This list is not exhaustive. It is a starting place.

Questions:
Is good character being taught?
Is it a visible curriculum? If it is, are there lesson plans?
If there is a curriculum, how is it evaluated?
Should character education be taught within the existing curriculum or does it need to be a stand alone effort?
Who should teach character education?
How can the school interface with the family?

These are just of few of the questions that need to be addressed. Once individuals agree to begin the dialogue, the concerns, and other questions and answers will quickly emerge. What is important is that the discussion take place.

Character education is not only about what is happening in classrooms. Character education in schools is but one element. No matter how effective or wide-spread school based character education programs are, they will have little lasting impact unless citizens include in this discourse other societal factors that impact children's moral development. For example, communities must discuss some of the following issues:

What is the effect on children's character development as the result of presentations of violence, crime, abusive use of alcohol and indiscriminate sex as presented in movies, television productions, advertisements, music and other media that are shown to or available to young children?

Does an arcade or PC video game depicting graphic violence as a problem-solving tool effect the character development of children?

What effect does the marketplace have on the development of values? Does saturation advertising shape behavior? Can the same advertising techniques used to convince consumers to buy products be used with children to get them to buy into respect and responsibility?

There are many more questions or concerns that need to be addressed as families and communities plan for the future of their children.

In the preface to *The Content of America's Character: Recovering Civic Virtue*, Eberly states,

> *"America's new frontiers lie in the realm of social change and girding up the institutions that impart character....Fortunately, the movement to restore character is finding a vast field of common ground, even in a society riddled with deep disagreement over politics and public policy.*
>
> *Transmitting values has always been the work of civilization. This means that an entire society must take the enterprise seriously."* [22]

As we enter the 21st Century it appears that people are taking the need to return to systematic, on purpose, character education seriously. The signs are clear. We are emerging from a value free or value neutral educational system. The prospects are good that this trend will continue to accelerate.

One of the most important elements, in this movement to restore common core values, is the common denominator, the school. The school not only has the opportunity to instill good character, it has the responsibility. In collaboration with other institutions and individuals the teachers of this nation can stem the tide of incivility and help create a new generation of trustworthy, respectful, responsible, fair, caring and accountable citizens.

The authors wish that a magic wand could be waved and the family could be restored to some ideal that may have existed in the past. This will not happen. Times have changed.

In February 1996 a junior high school student walked into a classroom at his school and shot to death the teacher and two fellow students.

This did not occur in the depths of the inner city where, for many youngsters, social problems and pressures are the norm. It happened in small town America.

If we, as parents, educators and community members don't solve this character deficit problem, we are doomed to live with the consequences. If we think that teen pregnancy, gangs, drug and alcohol abuse, school failure, a loss of civility, the lack of work ethic and violence are the problem, then we are doomed to live with these symptoms.

The problem is the lack of a moral compass, failure to instill values and expecting someone else to solve the problem. There is an illness in our society and we no longer can treat the symptom.

We, all of us, must start to cure the illness by going after the cause. Call it the teaching of the First R-Responsibility, moral education, values, ethics or character education. However this effort is labeled, the fact remains; if we are to rid ourselves of the illness, we must inoculate the emerging generation with good character. **Good character is taught not caught.**

Recap

1. Character education is catching on across the country in both public and private schools.
2. Both the educational community and the public at large are becoming aware that something must be done to solve our societal problems.
3. The awareness that we need to look toward character education goes beyond the "quick fix" attitude that generally deals with the symptoms, not the cause.
4. Community based character education is having a positive effect in several communities.
5. Character and values can and should be taught in a systematic, "on purpose" manner.

APPENDIX A

The Character Education Project
Los Angeles Unified School District

The current survey was designed by California Survey Research as a pilot study for the Jefferson Center For Character Education in cooperation with the Los Angeles Unified School District, to gather data on various discipline problems in the schools, and to learn the opinions of school administrators in the District toward the Los Angeles Unified School District's Value Education Project. In all, thirty-one schools participated in the survey at the beginning of the Fall 1990 semester. Twenty-five of the schools in the Los Angeles Unified School District Project were interviewed at the end of the Spring 1991 semester. Following are the key findings from the survey.

- All forms of reported discipline problems decreased from the academic year before the start of the program (the Fall 1990 semester) to the end of the first year of the program (the Spring 1991 semester). The biggest drop in discipline problems was in the number of tardy students sent to the office each month (40% decrease), followed by the number of students sent to the office for minor disciplinary problems (39% decrease), and major disciplinary problems, such as fighting, drugs, or weapons (25% decrease).
- Coinciding with a decrease in the number of disciplinary problems, the median level of student participation in extracurricular activities increased slightly from the Fall 1990 semester to the Spring 1991 semester, as did the median number of students on the Principal's Honor roll.

- Administrators reported an increase in student morale from the Fall 1990 semester to the Spring 1991 semester, but a slightly lower teacher morale for the same period.
- School administrators said parents were more involved in their children's education in the Spring 1991 semester than in the Fall 1990 semester. The increase in parental involvement was reported both at the school and in the home.
- The level of student responsibility increased from the Fall 1990 semester to the Spring 1991 semester. The administrators said that the students in their schools acted more responsibly, did not blame others, resisted peer pressure, and in general understood the concepts of respect, honesty and responsibility more in the Spring 1991 semester than in the Fall 1990 semester.
- The benefits of teaching values systematically were rated higher at the end of the Spring 1991 semester than at the beginning of the Fall 1990 semester. An overwhelming majority of the administrators in both the Fall 1990 semester and the Spring 1991 semester believe that the teachers in their schools should spend more time teaching values to the students.
- Overall, the program exceeded the expectations of the administrators in reducing discipline problems, and providing the opportunity to teach values. Specifically, the administrators said the program achieved more than they anticipated, particularly citing better school-wide morale and cohesiveness, improved student awareness for their actions, a decrease in discipline problems, better student self discipline, an opportunity to teach values in the classroom, and a common reference point to solve conflicts.
- The two most frequently mentioned "best" features of the program were that the lessons were easy to implement and that the program provided a common language and value

system. Improved student-teacher communication, consistent themes, and the program should be available in Spanish, were some of the other comments made by the administrators.

Sampling Plan

The current survey was designed by California Survey Research for the Jefferson Center for Character Education, in cooperation with the Los Angeles Unified School District, to gather data on the various discipline problems in the schools, and to learn the opinions of school administrators in the District toward the Character Education Project. In all, thirty-one schools (23 elementary and 8 junior high-middle schools) were contacted by the Center at the beginning of the Fall 1990 semester for their participation in this survey. An advance letter was mailed by the Center to each school soliciting their cooperation in the survey. Enclosed with the letter was a sheet asking for basic school information, such as the number of students referred to the office for major and minor discipline problems. A similar letter was sent to the same schools at the end of the Spring 1991 semester. In all, twenty-five schools (20 elementary and 5 junior high-middle schools) who interviewed at the beginning of the Fall 1990 semester and who participated in the Character Education Project, were contacted at the end of the Spring 1991 semester.

Questionnaire

The questionnaire used in this survey was designed by California Survey Research. The same questionnaire was used for both the Fall 1990 semester and the Spring 1991 semester interviews. The Spring 1991 questionnaire also had additional questions about the percent of teachers in the school who implemented the Character Education Project, and the best feature of the program.

The first questions asked about the discipline problems in the school, such as tardies, suspensions, referrals to the office for disrespect, fighting, drugs or weapons. Next, the administrators were asked to rate, from very low to a very high, the current morale of the students and teachers, the involvement of parents at school and in the home, the level of responsibility students are taking for their behavior, resistance to peer pressure, and in general, the level of understanding of the concepts of respect, honesty, and responsibility. Then, the administrators were asked about the benefit of teaching values systematically in the school, and their expectations of the Character Education Project.

Survey Execution

All interviews were conducted in English by telephone by trained professional interviewers from the offices of California Survey Research. The Fall 1990 semester interviews were conducted from October 31, 1990 through January 8, 1991, The Spring semester interviews were conducted from June 5, 1991 through August 21, 1991. All interviews were scheduled in advance, and after the schools received a letter from The Jefferson Center eliciting their cooperation. The long period of time allocated to complete the interviews was dictated by the availability of the administrators, different start dates for the project, and the implementation of year-round schools.

Analysis of Results

All responses to the survey were entered on paper questionnaires. The open-ended responses from the questions about expectations and the best feature of the program were manually organized and coded. All survey questionnaires were then checked for clarity and completeness. The information from the questionnaires was then keyed for computer analysis due to the small sample size, tests for statistically significant differences between the Fall 1990 responses and the Spring 1991 responses were deemed inappropriate. All reported results in this report are based on frequency data from the two semesters. The percentages used in this report are based on the number of administrators answering each question with a response other than "Don't Know" or "Refused to Answer."

Conclusions

The results from the current survey, designed as a pilot study to assess the effectiveness of the Character Education Project, suggest that the program met the goals for the project by modifying the behavior of the students in the schools that implement the program. The major conclusions from the results of this survey are as follows:

First, even though this study used a small sample of schools, the evidence suggests a trend toward reduced discipline problems, because all forms of reported discipline problems decreased from the academic year before the program was implemented to the end of the first full academic year of the program. Major discipline problems, such as fighting, drugs, or weapons, decreased by nearly 25 percent in an average month. Minor discipline problems and tardy students decreased by nearly 40 percent in an average month. And, because the administrators in the survey were contacted, in advance, and asked to look up the number of reported problems, the data used in this survey represent the administrators best estimate of the situation at their respective schools.

Second, school administrators had certain expectations of the program before its implementation. For instance, prior to the start of the project, the administrators expected to gain a systematic and consistent approach for teaching values, achieve better school-wide morale and cohesiveness, and obtain improved student awareness and responsibility for their actions. These expectations were met and exceeded by the end of the Spring 1991 semester.

The more than 500 teachers surveyed at the conclusion of the Spring 1991 semester had, for the most part, positive comments about the program. Even though the teachers were not in as a good a position as the administrators to judge the school-wide level of discipline problems, the teachers did cite many of the same gains and best features of the program as the administrators. The teachers, for instance, liked the "how to" approach of the program, the teacher-friendly lessons, and the opportunity to help students take responsibility for their actions.

Next, even though the administrators believe in the benefit of teaching values, their involvement in the project seemed to strengthen their commitment toward teaching values systematically. In their open-ended comments about the program many administrators seemed to emphasize the ease of implementation of the program, and the common language and values systems the program provided.

Finally, the data from the administrators survey of the Character Education Project should be used as evidence to support the philosophy that teaching values in the schools is worthwhile and can possibly reduce some of the problems now faced in the schools. A larger sample and Spanish-language materials are needed to validate the impact of the Thomas Jefferson Center Values Project on a district-wide basis.

APPENDIX B

The Pittsburgh Study

The Value of Character: Summary examines the nature and effectiveness of the **STAR** character education program that has been widely adopted by school districts across the country. The **STAR** program of the Jefferson Center for Character Education is aimed toward fostering respect and responsibility in students and creating more positive school climates.

Two Pittsburgh foundations, the Scaife Family Foundation and the Vera I. Heinz Foundation, wanted an independent evaluation of the effectiveness of the Jefferson Center's STAR program in use in a number of Pittsburgh area schools.

Professors Judith McQuaide, Joyce Feinberg and Gaea Leinhardt with the University of Pittsburgh School of Education conducted the study. Data were collected during one academic year in the three elementary schools which serve very different populations (suburban, urban, and inner-city), and which are considered to be exemplars of **STAR** program use. The analysis focused on **STAR** lessons delivered to 5th graders on the grounds that students in their last year of elementary school would have been exposed to the **STAR** program the longest and would represent the most complete picture of what the program can do.

In their report, released in October 1994, the researchers state "Although teaching the concepts of good character to public school students is not new, the increase in attention focused on character education is a relatively recent phenomenon as school districts throughout the country add character education programs to the curriculum. This increase indicates that a growing number of educators perceive a need for such programs." "Attempts to determine the effectiveness of such programs," the report states, "are few and far between. ...with most program evaluations in this area coming primarily from the program developers themselves."

The professors' chose the **STAR** program because of its widespread acceptance and use in their local area as well as elsewhere throughout the country. In order to understand and evaluate how the program worked, the professors conducted extensive observations of the program in action, as well as in-depth interviews with students, teachers and school principals.

Data were collected from three very different schools which are not named to protect their right to confidentiality.

Answers were sought to the following questions:

1. What are the perceived needs for this program in each school?
2. What are the critical components of successful program use?
3. Does the program meet the local needs?
4. What are student's understandings of the program?

In all three schools, the **STAR** program was seen as being beneficial not only to the student but also to the adults who were expected to model the behaviors. From discussing the **STAR** program in faculty meetings to planning displays and lessons, to looking for good student behavior to recognize and reward, all adults in school found the **STAR** program concepts becoming part of their daily life helping to foster a positive attitude throughout the building.

The **STAR** program was seen as one important component of a comprehensive effort to teach social skills. Each school in our study also used other, similar programs. In each case, the **STAR** program was considered to be the foundation; other programs were seen as complementary, building upon and reinforcing **STAR** concepts.

The **STAR** program was seen by the teachers and principles as a language-based tool which, by providing a common vocabulary, supported their efforts to enhance appropriate student behavior. Improving student behavior was seen as a logical prerequisite to the goal of improving students' academic success.

A major strength of this program, according to school principals and teachers, is in its simplicity and ease of use. Materials are well developed and easy to follow. No additional preparation is necessary for teachers or principals, and the program can easily be integrated into the life of the school.

SCHOOL PERSONNEL REACTIONS

"The **STAR** program is a very positive program and I have been Very pleased with it; and I have seen success with it; and I firmly believe in it. I firmly believe that this is a need of the hour in public education. Oh, if we could just somehow really infuse this as never before in these kids. Get these kids before they go off the deep end."

"I see the **STAR** program as developing language, and through repetition, and through it being implemented and built into every discipline within the school, the kids get it no matter where they are. Our focus here is to develop a language within the child and because we believe that language affects attitudes and attitudes affect behavior. So I see all of that linking together, tied together."

"You're not pushing something else out of the curriculum. It is not time consuming: it's an attitude and it's a vocabulary change for some people."

"Teachers feel very comfortable implementing (**STAR**) because it is very simple... The program is planned; the banners are made; the posters are made. Scripts are there. It's appealing. The program is appealing enough to make you want to use it. It will meet the needs of the student; you will spend more time teaching after the program kicks in."

STUDENT REACTIONS

To determine whether or not students knew what the **STAR** program was all about, the researchers began by asking what the acronym "**STAR**" represents. Almost all students (28 out of 30) could state the phrase *Stop, Think, Act, Review.*

- Students answered this question with little or no hesitation. Such a high degree of recall suggests that this meaning for the **STAR** acronym has been very solidly learned by a large majority of students.
- Students were then asked if they actually practice the skill of stopping to think before acting. Responses were categorized as "yes," "no," and "sometimes."
- Only two students answered "no," that they did not stop to think before acting. Twelve students answered "yes" and sixteen answered "sometimes," they were also asked to give an example of a time when they did not stop to think before acting, or when they should have first stopped to think. All thirty students were able to give examples, demonstrating not only that they knew the slogan, but also that they had internalized the ideas of stopping to think before taking action.
- Fewer students recalled the underlying theme (Success Through Accepting Responsibility) as a meaning for the **STAR** acronym (11 out of 30 or 37%).
- Students were next asked for a word representing a monthly theme that they had discussed, in order to determine if they were familiar with, or remembered, any of the monthly **STAR** themes as well as to discover which concepts were most often recalled. 23 out of 30 students (approximately 77%) remembered at least one theme.
- Student answers to this question reflect most of the actual program themes: How can I be a **STAR**? How can I be kind and courteous? How can I make good choices? How can I

be of service to others? How can I show courage? How can I be honest and trustworthy? How can I show respect for myself and others? How can I carry out my commitments? How can I reward myself for being responsible? Thus, there seemed to be concrete evidence here of significant student internalization of the **STAR** program goals.

• To determine whether or not students were able to do the **STAR** actions, the researchers relied primarily on classroom observations and on students' self-reports during classroom discussions. Although the students in our study were not consistent models of ideal **STAR** behavior, there was a strong sense that they did try to enact appropriate behavior and that the frequent discussion helped to focus their attention on the program goals. As the school year progressed and students came to know each other well, they exhibited an increased ability to respond sensitively and positively toward each other.

Conclusions

The research team reached the following conclusions:

The **STAR** program is carefully thought out and comprehensive, easy to use, and does not need to interfere with other curriculum demands.

Because the **STAR** program addresses what most would consider to be universal values, the program can meet the needs of diverse school situations and populations. Regardless of the size of the school or the nature of its student population, no one argues against the need for students to have a sense of respect, responsibility, concern for others, and for reinforcement of ethical behaviors. All of the school personnel we interviewed felt that the **STAR** program met their local needs.

One concern is finding ways to promote the program so that other principals will want to adopt and use it. Each principal knew of schools in which the program was not effective because of lack of commitment.

Overall, the findings indicated that the **STAR** program was a highly valued, language-based social skills program which had a strong positive influence on the behavior of students in each school in addition to the specific skills and themes of the **STAR** program, its ease of use and adaptability were significant to its success.

Excerpted from *THE VALUE OF CHARACTER: SUMMARY* by Judith McQuaide, Joyce Fienberg, and Gaea Leinhardt of the Learning Research & Development Center, University of Pittsburgh, Pittsburgh, PA 15260—October 1994

This research was supported in part by funds from the Scaife Family Foundation and the V. I. Heinz Foundation.

APPENDIX C

What Makes Character Education Programs Work?

Eleven elements are essential if character education programs are to improve student conduct and enrich the educational environment.

The bell rang at Limerick Elementary School in Canoga Park, California, and students made their way to the playground for lunch. A few minutes later, the daily line of disruptive youngsters began to form outside the principal's office. Long after the other students returned to their classrooms for the afternoon, the long line of students waiting to be disciplined or counseled for misbehavior remained.

Principal Ronni Ephraim ushered children in and out of her office. She reported that she "rarely had time to do more than ask what they did, tell them not to do it again, and dole out some form of discipline." She added, "I rarely talked with the children, especially those who really needed my attention."

Fortunately, this scenario was being played out at Limerick School at the same time that the Jefferson Center for Character Education was identifying schools in the Los Angeles Unified School District (LAUSD) that were willing to pilot a character education program. The Jefferson Center had developed a curriculum that had proven successful in other schools and wanted to demonstrate its effectiveness in a cross-section of elementary and middle schools in the sprawling Los Angeles megalopolis. LAUSD, for its part, hoped that the character education program would improve student conduct and enrich the educational environment.

Key Elements for Effective Programs

Past experiences in schools in St. Louis, Pittsburgh, Honolulu and elsewhere provided strong evidence that character education programs could be quite effective when key criteria in developing and implementing the curriculum were met. In fall 1990, Limerick and 24 other LAUSD schools initiated a program that included the following elements:

Direct instruction. Schools cannot assume that the language, concepts, behaviors, and skills of good character are written into the genetic code; learned at home, from television, or in the neighborhood; or absorbed through the invisible hand of the general curriculum. Like arithmetic, as "responsibility" and "respect" must be purposeful and direct. Students should hear and see the words, learn their meanings, identify appropriate behaviors, and practice and apply the values. Direct instruction builds a foundation for more advanced learning infused throughout the general curriculum; even then, direct instruction is necessary for infusion to be focused and effective.

Language-based curriculum. Children entering the schools today often lack the vocabulary for understanding basic value concepts such as "honesty" and "courage." Even when they can define such values, they often fail to connect them to their own behavior. Successful character education programs focus students' attention on the basic language that expresses core concepts and links the words to explicit behavior.

For example, at Newcomb School in Long Beach, California, students in Anna Wood's 3rd grade class learned the meaning of "courage." Then, in cooperative learning groups, they developed lists of the ways in which children can demonstrate courage in the classroom. One group decided that students could show courage by "being nice to kids that other kids tease."

Positive Language. Students must know what is expected of them if they are to practice appropriate behavior. Therefore, common negative language such as "Don't be late" or "Don't forget your pencil" should be translated into explicit positive language as in "Be on time" or "be prepared."

At Bellerive School in the Parkway School District in St. Louis County, Missouri, a new teacher was often heard telling her students, "Don't get out of your seat," "Don't get up to look out the window," and "Don't wander around the classroom." Finally, a veteran teacher advised her to "tell the kids exactly what you want them to do." The next day, the new teacher firmly told her students to "Sit down!" To her amazement, they did.

Content and process. In addition to teaching the content of consensus and civic values, and effective character education curriculum should provide a process for implementing those values when making decisions. At Parmalee Elementary School in Los Angeles, Students are taught that honesty is better than dishonesty, being on time is better than being late, being polite is better than being rude. Building on this content, students learn a four-step process that teaches them to examine alternatives and consequences and then assess whether their choices are likely to bring them closer to goals such as personal and social responsibility. As students learn and practice the decision-making process, they develop the skills needed for making ethical choices.

Visual reinforcement. Character education is in competition with adverse desires, messages, and pressures in our society. The visual presentation of character values is, in effect, an advertising campaign intended to keep the words, concepts, and behaviors learned in the class at the forefront of students' attention. Visual displays illustrate and reinforce good character. Thus, when students and staff traverse the hallways of Santa Barbara Junior High School in Santa Barbara, California, they encounter 4' × 8' silver and blue "character" signs hanging from the ceilings. The main hallway is adorned by a huge banner that prominently displays the word RESPECT.

School climate approach. Effective character education should spill over the boundaries of the classroom into the playground, the office, the cafeteria, the bus, and then into the home and neighborhood. This school climate approach generates a common language and culture that fosters positive peer recognition and encourages all members of the school community to exemplify and reward behavior consistent with core values and ethical decision making.

During "Be Polite" month at the Bellerive School, the first thing that staff, students, and visitors see when they enter the building is a large calendar, which lists a different way to be polite for each day of the month. On the third day of the month, for example, everyone is reminded to be polite "by listening when others are speaking."

Teacher-friendly materials. Teachers must be able to implement the character education curriculum with limited training and preparation. They should not have to write lengthy lesson plans, prepare student handouts, search out supplementary materials, or decode impossibly complex instructional manuals. Keeping curriculum materials simple and straightforward greatly increases the probability that the lessons will get taught consistently and effectively. Otherwise, teachers are likely to perceive systematic character education as an "add-on" rather than as an essential component of their teaching mission.

Teacher flexibility and creativity. Teachers not only need a basic framework to work with, but they also should be able to adjust character education lessons to individual teaching and learning styles. A successful character education curriculum is sufficiently flexible to allow teachers to exercise creativity in addressing special classroom circumstances while still adhering to school wide standards. Thus, one teacher may have the class designate four or five ways to practice tolerance while another teacher may decide to have individual students select a specific tolerant behavior for practice. The teachers' approaches may vary even though the same language and concepts are taught in both classrooms.

Student participation. Character education is most effective when students develop a sense of ownership. It is not enough to tell students how to behave. They must participate in the process of framing goals in order to achieve them. At the Kauluwela School in Honolulu, Hawaii, each student in Leona Englehart's 5th grade class decides on individual character goals and how to met them. Typical individual goals include, "I will be on time," "I will do all my homework," or "I will be polite to classmates." Each student writes his or her name and goal on a cutout of a foot. The cutouts are then placed on the classroom wall in an ascending pattern that represents the "Steps to Success." Students develop a sense of ownership because they have chosen the goals and means for achieving them.

Parental involvement and then some. Character education programs are most effective and enduring when the school routinely confers with parents, lets them know what is being taught, and involves them in the curriculum. Corona del Mar High School in Newport Beach, California, kicked off its "Respect and Responsibility" program by hosting a Character Education Day that drew together school board members, administrators, teachers, students, parent groups, and community leaders to discuss local needs and goals. Bellerive School helped to sustain and enrich its character education program, first by keeping parents informed of the "theme of the month," and then by providing suggestions regarding how parents could encourage theme-appropriate behavior at home.

Evaluation. Implementation of a character education program must include a pre-assessment of goals, occasional consultation during the program, and then a post-evaluation of results. In the planning stages, school staff members should clearly articulate their expectations and explicitly detail the various goals they hope to accomplish. As they implement the program, periodic meetings will help teachers to keep goals in mind and adapt classroom lessons accordingly. Finally, the program evaluation should assess the outcomes in terms of anecdotal reports from teachers ("My students seem to be more responsible.") and appropriate data on measurable changes in key variables (Have absences decreased? Are office referrals down? Do more students make the honor role?).

Implementation Leads to Results

The staff at Limerick School decided to participate in the Jefferson Center-LAUSD pilot project by implementing a character education curriculum that contains the 11 elements described above. Some teachers approached the pilot with an air of pessimism. The veterans had tried "savior" programs over the years and had become somewhat cynical. Nonetheless, they moved forward. Within three months, they were reporting positive changes in classroom behavior. Ronni Ephraim noticed that the lunchtime line outside her office was getting shorter. At the end of the school year, she reported that "the line was gone." Indeed, only three or four students per day were being referred to her. "Those who were sent to the office really needed to be helped. Now I have time to work with them."

The effectiveness of character education at Limerick School was not unique. At the 25 elementary and middle schools completing the Jefferson Center-LAUSD pilot during the 1990-91 school year, major discipline problems decreased by 25 percent; minor discipline problems went down 39 percent; suspensions fell by 16 percent; tardiness dropped by 40 percent; and unexcused absences (which often translates into lost revenue) declined by 18 percent. In addition, surveyed teachers generally felt that students did learn to take greater responsibility for their behavior and school work while principals reported a noticeable increase in the number of students on their honor rolls. Schools are, essentially, a community of their own. If the whole school community fosters the language, culture, and climate of good character, then the students who spend a significant portion of their time there will acquire the words, concepts, behaviors, and skills that contribute to good conduct, ethical decision making, and a fertile learning environment.

The above article is reprinted from **Educational Leadership** the journal of the Association of Supervision and Curriculum Development. November 1993. B. David Brooks and Mark E. Kann, authors.

BIBLIOGRAPHY

CHAPTER 1

1. "Troubled Teenagers," *U. S. News & World Report,* December 14,1981, p. 40.
2. James S. Coleman, news release by *Character, Inc.,* Chicago, December 7, 1981.
3. Socrates, quoted in *Education in Upheaval 21,* no. 18.
4. William H. Blanchard, "Coping with Man's Violence," *Los Angeles Times,* April 16, 1972.
5. *To Establish Justice, to Insure Domestic Tranquillity, final report on Causes and Prevention of Violence,* Washington, D.C., December, 1969, p. xxi.
6. David Bazelon, speech to Western Society of Criminology, 1981.
7. Arthur Shenfield, "The Failure of Socialism, Learning from the Swedes and English," *Critical Issues* (Washington, D.C.: Heritage Foundation, 1980), pp. 19, 20.
8. Warren E. Burger, *Annual Report to the American Bar Association,* Houston, February 8, 1981.
9. Walter Lippmann, "Education Versus Western Civilization," address at annual meeting of American Association for the Advancement of Science, December 29, 1940. In *American Scholar* (Spring 1941).
10. John A. Howard, "Rediscovering Joy," *Bohemian Grove Lakeside Talk,* July 24, 1973, p. 3.
11. George C. S. Benson and Thomas S. Engeman, *Amoral America* (1975; rev. ed., Durham, N.C.: Carolina Academic Press, 1982).
12. Ibid., pp. 27, 224, 225

CHAPTER 2

1. Andrew Oldenquist, " 'Indoctrination" and Societal Suicide," *Public Interest,* no. 63 (Spring 1981):81.
2. W. D. Humbly, "Origins of Education Among Primitive Peoples, 1926," cited in F. Eby and C. Flinn Arrowood, *The History and Philosophy of Education Ancient and Medieval* (1940). p. 15
3. Maurice Connery, "DUI Tieline," DUI Demonstration Program funded by California Office of Traffic Safety, no. 6, January 1980, p. 3.
4. John R. Silber, "The Gods of the Copy Book Headings: Reflections on the No-Fault Life," address at the 17th Anniversary Banquet of the Jefferson Center for Character Education, November 25, 1980.
5. George C. S. Benson and Thomas S. Engeman, *Amoral America* (1975; rev. ed., Durham, N.C.: Carolina Academic Press, 1982), p. 25.
6. Reed J. Irvine, "Why Not Try Teaching Moral Precepts Again," *Sunday Star* (Washington, D.C.), April 9, 11967
7. Lenore Romney, Meeting sponsored by National Center for Voluntary Action, Frederick, Md., May 16, 1972
8. Larry Jensen and Holly Passey, "Moral Education Curricula in the Public Schools," *Religion & Public Education* 1,2,3, (1993):28
9. Ibid., pp. 186, 187.
10. Ibid. p. 11.
11. Ibid. p. 185.
12. Ibid. p. 186, 187.
13. Robert Hutchins, *The Human Dialogue,* p. 322.
14. Robert F. Peck with Robert J. Havighurst and Ruth Cooper, Jesse Lilienthal, and Douglas More, *The Psychology of Character Development,* (New York: John Wiley & Sons, 1960), p. 189

15. Abraham H. Maslow, "Some Education Implications of the Humanistic Psychologies," *Harvard Educational Review* (Fall 1968):1
16. Abraham H. Maslow, "Music Education and Peak-Experiences," *Music Educators Journal* (1968).
17. Abraham H. Maslow, *The Psychology of Science* (New York: Harder & Row, 1966) p. 133.

CHAPTER 3

1. Sandrah L. Pohorlak, "The Status of the Teaching of Moral and Spiritual Values in the Public Schools of the United State, Territories and Possessions" (Masters Thesis, University of Southern California, 1967) pp. 13,14.
2. Edwin F. Klotz, "Guidelines for Moral Instruction in California Schools," California State Department of Education, May 9, 1969, p. 24.
3. George C. S. Benson and Thomas S. Engeman, *Amoral America* (1975; rev. ed., Durham, N.C.: Carolina Academic Press, 1982), pp. 182, 183.
4. Walter Lippmann, "Education Versus Western Civilization," address at annual meeting of American Association for the Advancement of Science, December 19, 1940.
5. Benjamin D. Wood, memorandum to Frank Goble, July 23, 1966.
6. Klotz, op cit., p. 7.
7. Donald Thomas and Rafael Lewy, "Education and Moral Conduct: Re-Discovering America," *Character 1*, no. 4 (January 1980).
8. Lawrence Kohlberg, "Teaching Virtues," *Ethics Education* (Winter 1971).
9. David Elton Trueblood, General Philosophy (New York: Harper & Row, 1963), p. 261.
10. Louis E. Raths, "What I Believe About Character Education," *Character Education Journal* (Fall 1972).

11. William J. Bennett and Edwin J. Delatre, "Moral Education in the Schools," *Public Interest* (Winter 1978): 82.

12. Ibid., p. 85.

13. Lawrence Kohlberg, "Stages of Moral Development as a Basis for Moral Education," *Moral Education: Interdisciplinary Approaches,* ed. Clive Beck et al. (Toronto: University of Toronto Press, 1971), p. 71.

14. Lawrence Kohlberg and E. Turiel, *Moralization Research, the Cognitive-Developmental Approach* (New York: Holt, Rinehart, & Winston, 1975).

15. Richard A. Baer, Jr., "Parents, Schools and Value Clarification," *Wall Street Journal,* April 12, 1982.

16. Reo M. Christenson, "Clarifying Values Clarification for the Innocent," *Christianity Today,* April 10, 1981, p. 3.

17. Thomas Lickona, *Educating for Character: How Our Schools Can Teach Respect and Responsibility* (Bantam Books, New York) 1991, p. 11, 12.

CHAPTER 4

1. Edwin F. Klotz, "Guidelines for Moral Instruction in California Schools," California State Department of Education, May 9, 1969, p. 5.

2. David Lawrence, "Teaching of Morality Has Not Been Tabooed," *U. S. News & World Report,* February 13,1967, p. 112.

3. Stephen Arons, "The Separation of School and State: *Pierce* Reconsidered," *Harvard Educational Review* 46, no. (February 1976).

4. George B. de Huszar, Henry W. Littlefield, and Arthur W. Littlefield, eds., *Basic American Documents* (Ames, Iowa: Littlefield, Adams, 1953), p. 66.

5. *The Writings of Thomas Jefferson,* ed. Paul Leicester Ford vols. (New York: G. P. Putnam's Sons, 1892-99):227.

6. Jonathan Elliot, ed., *The Debates in the Several State Conventions in the Adoption of the Federal Constitution,* 5 vols. (Philadelphia: J. B. Lippincott, 1901), 3:536-37.
7. William V. Wells, *The Life and Public Services of Samuel Adams,* 3 vols. (Boston: Brown & Company, 1865), 3:175.
8. Adrienne Koch, ed., *The American Enlightenment* (New York: George Braziller, 1965), p. 77.
9. Values Education Commission, Maryland, "Statement of Purpose," July 30, 1979.
10. Stephen H. Sachs, Report to Values Education Commission, Maryland, July 1979.
11. Daniel Callahan and Sissela Bok, "The Role of Applied Ethics in Learning," *Change* (Hildref Publications, Washington, D.C.) (September 1979).
12. Terrel H. Bell, speech at National Conference for Education and Citizenship, Kansas City, Mo., September 23, 1976; reprinted in *Jefferson Research Letter,* no. 134, May 1977.
13. State of California Education Code, Section 44806, "Duty Concerning Instruction of Pupils Concerning Morals, Manners and Citizenship."
14. Michigan State Board of Education, "Resolution," March 13, 1968.
15. Sandrah L. Pohorlak, "The Status of the Teaching of Moral and Spiritual Values in the Public Schools of the United States, Territories and Possessions" (Master's thesis, University of Southern California, 1967), p. 21.

CHAPTER 5

1. Thomas D. Haire, "Street Gangs: Some Suggested Remedies for Violence and Vandalism," *Police Chief* (Los Angeles), July 1979, p. 55.
2. Sheldon and Eleanor Glueck, "A Decade of Research in Criminology: Stock-taking and a Forward Look," address at Annual Banquet of Harvard Voluntary Defenders, Harvard

University, April 15, 1963. Reprinted from *Excerpta Criminologica 3*, no (September/October 1963).

3. "Why Young People 'Go Bad,'" exclusive interview with Professor and Mrs. Sheldon Glueck of Harvard Law School, *U.S. News & World Report*, April 26, 1965, p. 56.

4. Sheldon and Eleanor Glueck, "Delinquents and Nondelinquents in Depressed Areas: Some Guidelines for Community Action," *Community Mental Health Journal 2*, no. 3 (Fall 1966):218.

5. "Children of Permissive Parents Most Likely to Take Drugs, Research Reveals," *National Enquirer*, October 1, 1972.

6. Paul Roazen, Freud: Political and Social Thought. (New York: Alfred A. Knopf, 1968), p. 103.

7. Richard H. Blum & Associates. *Horatio Alger's Children: The Role of the Family in the Origin and Prevention of Drug Risk* (San Francisco: Jossey-Bass, 1972), pp. 59-61.

8. Ibid., p. 305.

9. "Opinion Roundup," *Public Opinion 2*, no. 2 (American Enterprise Institute for Public Policy Research, Washington, D.C.) (March/ May 1979):36.

10. George C. S. Benson and Thomas S. Engeman, *Amoral America* (1975; rev. ed., Durham, N.C.: Carolina Academic Press, 1982), pp. 182, 183.

11. John F. Travers and Russell G. Davis, "A Study of Religious Motivation and Delinquency," *Journal of Educational Sociology* 20 (January 1961).

12. Fredric Wertham, "School for Violence, Mayhem in the Mass Media," in *Where Do You Draw the Line?* Victor B. Cline (Provo, Utah: Brigham Young University Press, 1974), p. 157. Reprinted by permission.

13. Ibid., p. 161.

14. "What Is TV Doing to America?" *U. S. News & World Report*, August 2,1982, p. 27.

15. Don E. Eberly, Building the Habitat of Character, *"The Content of American Character,"* (New York, Madison Books) 1995, p. 31.

16. Wertham, op. cit., *pp.* 164, 173, 174.

17. Brown & Singhal, Influencing the Character of Entertainment: Ethical Dilemmas of Prosocial Programming in *"The Content of American Character,"* (New York, Madison Books) 1995, p. 333.

18. Ibid. p. 335.

19. Sandrah L. Pohorlak, "The Status of the Teaching of Moral and Spiritual Values in the Public Schools of the United State, Territories and Possessions" (Masters Thesis, University of Southern California, 1967) pp. 13,14.

20. Mark W. Cannon, "The Critical role of Principles in Strengthening Society's Value System." NASSP Bulletin 65, No. 448 (Reston, VA.) (November, 1981): 82

21. Richard Gorsuch, "Teacher and Pupil Values in the Elementary Schools," *Character Education Journal* (Fall 1972):20.

22. U. Bronfenbrenner, *Two Worlds of Childhood* (New York: Russell Sage, 1970).

23. Ellwood P. Cubberley, *Public Education in the United States* (1947).

24. John Dewey, *Democracy and Education* (New York: Free Press, 1966), p. 359.

25. Edwin F. Klotz, "Guidelines for Moral Instruction in California Schools," California State Department of Education, May 9, 1969, p. 24.

26. "National Education Association Research Memo," NEA Research Division of the National Education Association, Washington, D.C., November 1963.

27. Ibid.

28. Ibid

29. Ibid.

CHAPTER 6

1. Lewis Mayhew, from address given when he became president of the Association of Higher Education.
2. Los Angeles Unified School District, Instructional Planning Division, *The Teaching of Values*, Publication number GC-56, 1978.
3. Josephson, The Joseph and Edna Josephson Institute of Ethics. From promotional information regarding the CHARACTER COUNTS! Coalition. Marina del Rey, CA 1994
4. Ibid.
5. Ibid.

CHAPTER 7

1. Edwin F. Klotz, "Guidelines for Moral Instruction in California Schools," California State Department of Education, May 9, 1969, p. 5.
2. Herbert C. Mayer, "The Good American Program—A Teacher's Guide to the Direct Teaching of Citizenship Values in the Viewpoint, 1964).
3. Sheldon and Eleanor Glueck, *Delinquency in the Making* (New York: Harper & Row, 1952).
4. Hartshorne, M. A. May, and F. K. Shuttleworth, *Studies in the Organization of Character* (New York: Macmillan Co., 1930).
5. Robert F. Peck with Robert J. Havighurst and Ruth Cooper, Jesse Lilienthal, and Douglas More, *The Psychology of Character Development*, (New York: John Wiley & Sons, 1960), p. 189.
6. D. Satnick, *The Jefferson Center-Los Angeles Unified School District Values Education Project*. California Survey Research, Van Nuys, CA 1991.

CHAPTER 8

1. Character Education Task Force, "A Reawakening: Character Education and the Role of the School Board Member," California School Boards Association, August 1982, pp. 2,3.
2. Task force Report on *Student Violence and Vandalism,* California Schools Bards Association, September 1980, p. 4
3. Character Education Task Force, op. cit., p. 4.
4. Hebert C. Mayer, "The Good American Program-A Teacher's Guide to the Direct Teaching of Citizenship Values in the Elementary Grades" (New York: American Viewpoint, 1964)
5. Ibid., p. 14
6. Ibid., p. 3
7. California State Department of Education, *Caught in the Middle,* Report of the State Superintendent's Middle Grade Task Force. 1987
8. Thomas Lickona, *Educating for Character: How Our Schools Can Teach Respect and Responsibility* (Bantam Books, New York) 1991, p. 11, 12.
9. Young People's Press, *Lessons in Character,* (San Diego, Ca.). 1995.
10. John R. Silber, "The Gods of the Copy Book Headings: Reflections on the No-Fault Life," address at the 17th Anniversary Banquet of the Jefferson Center for Character Education, November 25, 1980.
11. George C.S. Benson and Thomas S. Engeman, *Amoral America.* (1975; rev. ed., Durham, N.C.; Carolina Academic Press, 1982), p. 175.
12. Reed J. Irvine, "Why Not Try Teaching Moral Precepts Again," *Sunday Star* (Washington, D.C.), April 9, 1967

CHAPTER 9

1. Solveig Eggerz, "Why Our Public Schools Are Failing and What We Must Do About It" (New Rochelle, N.Y.: America's Future, 1982).

2. William, Kilpatrick, "*Why Johnny Can't Tell Right From Wrong.* (New York, N.Y.; Touchstone), 1993

3. William J. Bennett and Edwin J. Delatre, "Moral Education in the Schools," *Public Interest* (Winter 1978): 82

4. Ibid., p. 83..

5. Ibid., p. 83

6. Eggerz, op. cit.

7. Howard Flieger, "Newcomer on Campus" *U. S. News & World Report,* September 29, 1975, p. 92.

8. Marvin Stone, "Are Ethics on the Way Back?" *U. S. News & World Report,* January 22, 1979, p. 80.

9. "Troubled Teenagers" *U. S. News & World Report,* December 15, 1981

10. "Building Character in the Public Schools: "Troubled Teenagers" *U. S. News & World Report,* Strategies for Success," National School Boards Association, NSBA Leadership Report, 1987-2, 1987, Forward

11. "Moral and Civic Education and Teaching About Religion," California State Board of Education, 1991

12. "Teaching Values and Ethics," American Association of School Administrators, AASA Critical Issues Series, 1991

13. Terry Eastland, "Teaching Morality in the Public Schools," *Wall Street Journal,* February 22, 1982, p. 24

14. "Girl Scouts Survey on the Beliefs of Moral Values of America's Children" Girl Scouts of the United States of America, 1989, p. 103.

15. "The Moral Life of America's Schoolchildren." Special Report, *Teacher Magazine,* March 1990, p. 41.

16. "It's Elementary," California State Department of Education, 1992, p. vii.

17. Ibid, p. 21

18. Charles C. Haynes, "Finding Common Ground," The Freedom Forum First Amendment Center, Vanderbilt University, (Nashville, TX.) 1994, p. ix.

19. Ibid, p. 14-10.
20. Henry A. Huffman, *Developing a Character Education Program: one school districts experience.* (ASCD Publications, Alexandria, VA), 1994
21. B. David Brooks, Community Based Character Education, *"The Context of America's Character,"* (Madison Books, Lanham, Md.) Commonwealth Foundation, 1995.
22. Don E. Eberly, *"The Content of America's Character,"* (Madison Books, Lanham, Md.) Commonwealth Foundation, 1995, p. 237.

Index

ORDER FORM

Please send me:

____ Copies of softcover edition @ $11.95 per copy   _____

____ Copies of hardcover edition @ $18.95 per copy _____

California residents add 8.25% tax   _____

Postage and handling for one copy $2.00

Postage and handling for additional
copies @ 75¢ each   _____

TOTAL ENCLOSED   _____

SHIP TO:

NAME _____

ADDRESS _____

CITY_____ STATE _____ ZIP_____

Please make checks payable to:

JEFFERSON CENTER FOR CHARACTER EDUCATION
2700 E. FOOTHILL BLVD.
#302
PASADENA, CA 91107
(818)792-8130, FAX (818) 792-8364